The Teletubbies Craft Book

The Teletubbies™ Craft Book

25 PROJECTS FOR ADULTS TO MAKE AND CHILDREN TO ENJOY

Gina Moore

TED SMART

For Flynn, my fiercest Teletubby critic

Photography by Shona Wood

This edition produced for The Book People Ltd, Hall Wood Avenue, Haydock, St Helens WA11 9UL by BBC Books an imprint of BBC Worldwide Publishing, BBC Worldwide Limited, Woodlands, 80 Wood Lane, London W12 0TT

First published in 1998 by BBC Worldwide Ltd
Woodlands, 80 Wood Lane, London, W12 0TT

ISBN 0 563 38462 X

Co-creators Teletubbies: Anne Wood and Andrew Davenport

Commissioning Editor: Viv Bowler
Project Editor Teletubbies: Sally Foord-Kelcey
Project Editor Craft Book: Emma Callery
Art Director: Ellen Wheeler
Designer: Janet James

Set in Bembo and Syntax
Printed and bound in Great Britain by Butler & Tanner Limited, Frome & London
Colour reproductions by Radstock Repro Limited, Midsomer Norton
Papercase printed by Lawrence Allen Ltd, Weston-Super-Mare.

The author and publisher takes no responsibility for any injury or loss arising from the procedures and materials described in this book. Materials, tools, skills and work areas vary greatly and are the responsibility of the reader. Follow the manufacturers' instructions and take the appropriate safety precautions.

Contents

Introduction   6

Teletubby Toys and Gifts   9

Teletubbies in Motion   10
Greetings from Teletubbyland   12
Teletubbies on my Fingers   16
Tubbytronic Launchpad   18
The Sun Photoframe   24
Tubby Toast and Custard Splat
        Fridge Magnets   27
Tubby Toast Countdown Calendar   30
Tubby Dice Stool   35
Tubbytronic Superdome Cake   40

Teletubbyland   45

Teletubby Snuggledown   46
Tubby Bye-byes   52
Tubbytronic Window Blind   56
Tubby Table Mat   61
Follow the Flag Stencilled Wall Frieze   62
Hide-and-seek Pockets   68
Laa-Laa's Rag Rug   72

Teletubby Wear   77

Tubbied T-shirts   78
Tubby Aerial Hats   80
Dipsy's Hat   86
Po's Back Pack   90
Tubbytronic Rain Capes   94
Tinky Winky's Bag and
        Tubby Toast Purse   100
Custard Splats on my Toes   105
Teletubby Tutu   106
Tubby Custard Protectors   108

Templates   112
Useful Addresses   118
Author's Acknowledgments   119

Introduction

My first introduction to the Teletubbies was when my four-year-old son surprised me by breaking off from the usual fighting game with one of his friends, to cry 'Big hug'. The two little boys then embraced passionately. It was some time before I realised that this was not solely due to the sensitive upbringing I was giving him. Unbeknown to me, he had been Tubbied.

Much has been written about the enormously wide appeal of the Teletubbies, and I don't want to add to that. However, what struck me from the beginning is the way the Teletubbies live in an entirely child-friendly environment where no adults tell them what to do or how to respond. I have tried hard to carry that through to the projects in this book so that, even though this is primarily a book for adults, the projects it includes have, first and foremost, to have child-appeal.

Where possible I have included projects such as the Tubby Table Mat (page 61), the Tubbied T-shirts (page 78) and the custard-splattered shoes (page 105), in which children themselves can be involved. Even where the skills needed are inevitably those of an adult,

such as those required to make the Tubby Dice Stool (page 35), the bed head cover (page 52) or Hide-and-seek Pockets (page 68), I have created articles that children will want to use and play with rather than things that are merely decorative.

The Teletubbies Craft Book is divided into three sections: Toys and Gifts, Teletubbyland (things to make to turn your child's room into Teletubbyland) and Teletubby Wear. Each project has detailed written instructions as well as illustrations and photographs to help in their construction. Although inevitably some of the projects are easier than others, none of them requires specialist skills or materials. At the end of the book there is a section of Teletubby templates to trace or photocopy for use in the projects.

I hope this book will inspire you to design and make your own creations too. By making things that your children enjoy, you will be showing them the enduring qualities of making something yourself. In turn, this will encourage their own creativity, and what better way to start this trend than being accompanied by the Teletubbies: Tinky Winky, Dipsy, Laa-Laa and Po.

Gina Moore

Teletubby Toys and Gifts

Teletubbies in Motion

EVEN THE TINIEST new-born baby will be transfixed and stimulated by the silent motion of a colourful mobile so here's one made with beautiful hand-made paper and narrow satin ribbon that would be perfect hung above a baby's cot.

For the light padding, 2oz polyester wadding is sandwiched between two layers of delicate paper. This results in strong colours that nevertheless remain translucent and as light as air. You could, of course, make this mobile with any kind of paper or decide to use card in the right colours, and, if it's thicker and stronger, you could forget the wadding and stitching.

Making the shapes

1 Cut two 15cm (6in) square pieces of paper in all of the colours (except the grey and buff). Cut one 15cm (6in) square of wadding for each colour. Transfer a template of each Teletubby, one sun and four flower heads from pages 113-117 onto the sheets of paper in the appropriate colours. Use a slightly blunt pencil to avoid snagging the delicate paper.

2 Lay all the squares of paper wrong side up on a large sheet of newspaper and apply a fine spray of adhesive. Working quickly before the adhesive has time to dry, sandwich the sheets of paper over a layer of wadding. If you are not using adhesive, pin the sheets of paper on either side of the wadding but it will make stitching less straightforward.

3 With the sewing machine stitch set at a medium length for ease of control, stitch around the traced outlines. Then with the paper scissors, cut closely around the outline.

MATERIALS
- *translucent hand-made paper in red, purple, yellow, lime green, blue, pink and grey*
- *coloured paper in cream and buff*
- *15cm (6in) of 2oz polyester wadding*
- *blunt pencil*
- *art and craft spray adhesive (optional)*
- *sewing machine*
- *sharp paper scissors*
- *adhesive stick*
- *tweezers (optional)*
- *felt-tipped pens in brown and black*
- *2m (2yd) of narrow satin ribbon in red, purple, green and yellow*
- *2 green flower sticks*
- *green cotton*

4 Cut out faces and ears in buff and cream paper and glue into position using the tweezers, if necessary. Cut out tummy screens in grey paper and glue in position. Draw the faces with the appropriate coloured felt-tipped pen. It helps if you trace the features lightly in pencil first.

Assembling the mobile

1 Cut the satin ribbon to the following lengths: 1m (1yd) for each Teletubby, 30cm (12in) for each flower and 80cm (30in) for the sun. Choose whichever colour you feel is appropriate. Glue one end of each ribbon to the back of each item.

2 Cut the two flower sticks to 30cm (12in) and hold them together in the centre so they form a right-angled cross. Bind them securely together with a length of green cotton.

3 Tie the Teletubbies into position at either end of each stick so they dangle about 30cm (12in) below the sticks. Tie the flowers halfway along the sticks, dangling about 20cm (8in) below. Tie the sun to the centre of the sticks, about 10cm (4in) below. Trim the ribbons above the flowers, but run the other ribbons above the sticks. Hold them in your hand and adjust the lengths until the mobile is balanced and then tie them off tightly.

Greetings from Teletubbyland

A HANDMADE CARD always says more than its shop-bought counterpart. Here are some simple ideas that will convey your greetings with that personal touch. It is important to be accurate and precise with paper engineering and it really makes things easier if you have a craft knife with a supply of new blades and a steel ruler. A self-healing cutting mat is also helpful so that you don't have to worry about scratching the table. But it wouldn't be practical to invest in this equipment for a one-off card and it's possible to make any of these designs without one – make precise measurements and use a sharp pair of paper scissors. The holographic card included in these projects can easily be replaced with shiny sweet wrappers if you prefer.

Door Card

MATERIALS
- *thin card in silver, blue, pale green, dark green, white and the colour of your featured Teletubby (in this case, yellow for Laa-Laa)*
- *craft knife*
- *tiny piece of holographic card or other shiny paper*
- *art and craft spray adhesive or stick*
- *coloured paper in cream or buff*
- *fine-point felt-tipped pen in black*

1 Cut a piece of silver card 36 x 12.5cm (14 x 5in). With the wrong side up, score two foldlines 9cm (3½in) from either end. Carefully fold the ends in towards the centre along these scored lines. Transfer the petal-shaped window panes from page 42 onto the wrong side of the card at either end. Cut out the panes with a craft knife.

2 Cut a piece of blue card 18 x 12.5cm (7 x 5in) and stick it to the white side of the centre part of the silver card. Cut hill shapes out of pale and dark green card and stick them over the blue card. Cut a white cloud and stick that to the blue card. With the landscape in place and the card folded, draw and then cut a curved top to the card. Use a plate to help you get a good curve.

3 Transfer the Teletubby outline of your choice from pages 113 –116 onto the appropriate coloured card. Cut out the Teletubby and also cut a tummy screen out of holographic card (or other shiny paper stuck flat onto a layer of card) and a face and two ears out of the cream or buff paper. Draw or trace the features onto the face with the black felt-tipped pen. Stick the face, ears and screen into position. Stick the Teletubby down on the landscape.

13

Pop-up Card

MATERIALS
- *thin card in blue, dark green, white, pale green, and the colour of your featured Teletubby (in this case, purple and green for Tinky Winky and Dipsy)*
- *art and craft spray adhesive or stick*
- *felt-tipped pens in various colours*
- *tiny piece of holographic card or other shiny paper*
- *coloured paper in cream or buff*
- *fine-point felt-tipped pen in black*
- *glitter glue pen*

1 Cut a piece of blue card 30 x 13.5cm (12 x 5¼in). Score a fold line down the centre and fold in half.

2 Cut a piece of dark green card 22 x 13.5cm (8½ x 5¼in) and then cut an outline of hills along the top short edge. Lay it on the blue card and mark where the centre fold will come. Score that fold and then draw a hill outline below. Score another foldline along the base of the hill. Cut out the hill with a tab that extends above it as far as the distance between the foldlines. Score across the top and bottom of the tab. Fold along all the scored foldlines, making sure the folds across the top and bottom of the tab go the opposite way.

centre line

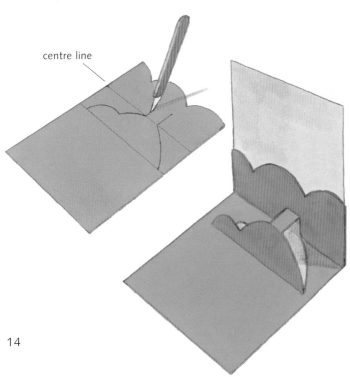

3 Stick the dark green card to the blue card, aligning the bottom edges and centre foldline. Cut two clouds out of white card and stick them to the blue card. Draw flat flowers onto the pale green card, colour them in and cut around them roughly. Stick onto the dark green card. Draw a plant with flowers onto the pale green card, colour it in and cut around it roughly. Stick it to the pop-up part of the hill, so that the flowers extend above the hill.

4 Transfer the Teletubby outlines of your choice from pages 113–116 onto the appropriate coloured cards. Cut them out and also cut out the tummy screens from holographic card (or shiny paper stuck flat onto a layer of card) and stick into position. Cut faces and ears out of the cream or buff coloured paper. Draw or trace the features onto the faces with the black felt-tipped pen. Stick the faces and ears into position. Stick the Teletubbies to the pop-up hill.

5 With a glitter glue pen draw a speech bubble on a piece of card and write 'eh-oh!' in it. Cut it out and glue it to the front of the card.

Sliding Tummy Card

MATERIALS
- *thin card in blue, pale green, white, dark green and the colour of the Teletubby you want to feature (in this case, red for Po)*
- *art and craft spray adhesive or stick*
- *coloured paper in cream or buff*
- *fine-point felt-tipped pen in black*
- *tiny piece of holographic card or other shiny paper*
- *snapshot of your recipient*
- *coloured felt-tipped pens*

|1| Cut a piece of blue card 37.5 x 15cm (15 x 6in). Divide it in three down its length and score down the card at these points so that it will fold easily and cleanly. Fold the card along both scored lines towards the wrong side.

|2| Cut a piece of pale green card 12.5 x 6cm (5 x 2¼in). To form a background of hills, draw and then cut a wavy line along one long edge. Stick it to the centre panel of the blue card with the bottom edges aligned. Cut out clouds of white card and stick them onto the blue card. Draw an outline of a group of flowers onto dark green card, colour it in and stick onto the pale green hill.

|3| Transfer the Teletubby outline of your choice from pages 113–116 onto the appropriately coloured card. Cut out a hole for a tummy screen. Cut a face and two ears out of cream or buff paper. Draw or trace the features onto the face with the black felt-tipped pen. Stick the face and ears in place.

|4| Half-way down the right-hand fold cut a 3.5cm (1½in) wide curved opening. Place the Teletubby on the card. To allow room for the slider to move easily, the Teletubby has to stand towards the right-hand side of the card with the tummy screen above the hills and aligned with the curved opening. Draw the tummy position onto the blue card and then cut it out. Stick down the Teletubby.

|5| Make a slider 10 x 3cm (4 x 1¼in) from green card. Draw an arrow head onto the right-hand end. Then cut a 2.5cm (1in) square of holographic paper (or other shiny paper stuck flat onto a layer of card). Cut two other 2.5cm (1in) squares of white card. On one, draw flowers and colour them in. On the other, stick a snapshot photograph of your recipient's face. If you haven't got one, draw a picture of him or her. Stick the squares towards the left-hand end of the slider neatly butted together in the order shown to the left.

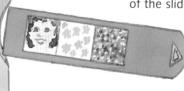

|6| Turn the card face down and open up. With the slider in position, stick two long pieces of card to the back to act as a guide for the slider. Apply glue to the top, side and bottom of the centre panel and stick the side with the slider over the slider mechanism. It is important not to get glue near the slider mechanism or you will find it will jam. So, if you are using art and craft spray adhesive, protect the centre with a spare piece of card.

15

Teletubbies on my Fingers

FINGER PUPPETS are much easier for very little hands to manoeuvre than glove puppets and will provide hours of creative story-telling. They are small enough to carry with you at all times to be brought out at moments of crisis to distract, for example, from the horrors of an injection or a visit to the dentist. Or keep them in the car so that they will be available to help while away a long journey. Even better, they are very quick and easy to make and if you fix them to a blank greetings card with some re-usable adhesive they make an imaginative and easily posted gift.

> **MATERIALS**
> - *squares or scraps of felt in red, yellow, lime green, purple, grey, beige and brown*
> - *matching sewing thread*
> - *fusible webbing*
> - *felt-tipped pen in black*
> - *embroidery silk in white and brown*

Making the puppets

1 Trace the templates of the finger puppets below onto paper and cut roughly around the outlines. Using the paper templates as a guide to size, cut two layers of felt in the appropriate colour and pin the paper template on top.

2 Stitch through the paper and both layers of felt following the outline of the template. Backstitch at the beginning and end of the stitching to secure. Tear the paper template away and trim the felt close to your stitchline.

Decorating the puppets

1 Trace the tummy screen, face, ears and eyes onto the smooth side of some fusible webbing. Cut roughly around them and iron onto the appropriate colours of felt. Cut them out carefully, peel off the backing and place in position on the felt body. Iron on carefully, following the manufacturer's instructions.

2 Draw pupils in each eye with the black felt-tipped pen. Embroider highlights in each eye with white embroidery silk, and a nose and mouth with brown embroidery silk.

Tubbytronic Launchpad

HERE IS SOMETHING to make up for the youngest Teletubby fans – a custard machine playmat holding hidden surprises. Designed to stimulate a baby's sense of touch and emerging curiosity, it is made using a variety of differently textured fabrics and hides a custard splat that crackles and Dipsy's hat that rattles, a mirror under a Velcroed flap and a buried squeaker.

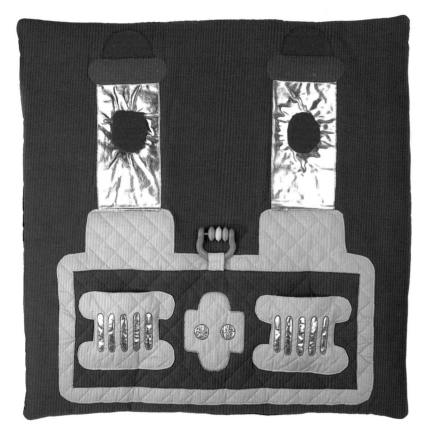

MATERIALS

- 1.25m (1¼yd) cotton jersey in royal blue
- 1m (1yd) strong fabric such as drill or corduroy
- 1cm (½in) squared paper
- felt-tipped pen in black
- 1.5m (1½yd) fusible webbing
- 20cm (8in) silver fabric
- thin white paper
- 50cm (½yd) quilted polycotton in pale pink
- contrast coloured sewing thread
- scraps of shocking pink, royal blue and black and white cow fun fur
- squeaker
- child's plastic mirror
- a small piece of Velcro
- hand-held rattle
- piece of cellophane
- empty Tic-tac box
- couple of dried beans
- 50cm (½yd) tape
- 1m (1yd) of 9oz polyester wadding
- pearlised silver fabric paint

Making the pockets

1 Cut background piece (**28**) 90cm (36in) square out of blue cotton jersey. Cut the underneath piece (**34**) the same size out of corduroy. Scale up the drawing on pages 22–3 (see page 112) and draw onto newspaper with a black felt-tipped pen.

2 Trace the shapes of pieces **1–10** onto the paper side of fusible webbing and iron onto the back of silver fabric. Cut them out. Trace the shape for pockets **11** and **12** onto a sheet of thin white paper and add a 1cm (½in) seam allowance all the way round. Cut this out and use it as a pattern to cut out four pocket pieces – two in pink quilted polycotton and two in blue cotton jersey. Peel the paper backing off the silver pieces **1–10** and iron them onto the right sides of the pink pockets. Satin stitch all around the edges with contrast coloured thread.

3 With right sides together pin one blue jersey pocket piece to one pink quilting pocket piece. Leaving a 1cm (½in) seam allowance, stitch around the edge stopping about 5cm (2in) before the point where you started. Pull the pocket right side out through this gap and sew up the gap by hand.

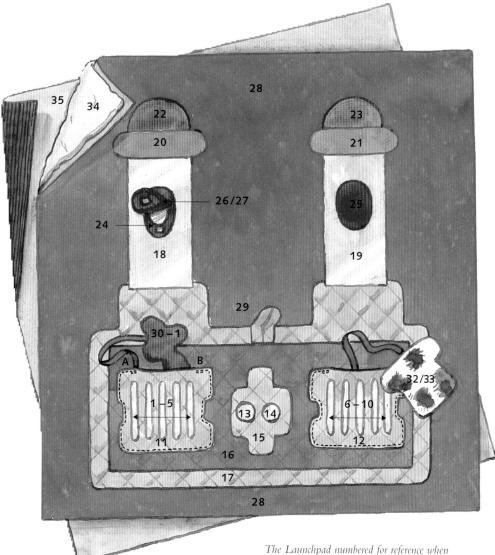

The Launchpad numbered for reference when
following the making instructions.

Making the custard machine

1 Trace the shapes of **13**, **14**, **15**, **16** and **17** onto the paper side of fusible webbing. Cut them out roughly and iron shapes **13** and **14** onto the wrong side of silver fabric, **15** and **17** onto the wrong side of pink quilted polycotton, and **16** onto the wrong side of blue cotton jersey. Cut them out neatly.

2 Peel the paper backing off **13** and **14** and iron into position on the right side of pink **15**. Leaving the paper backing on **15**, satin stitch with a contrast coloured thread around the circles. Peel the backing off **15** and iron into position in the centre of **16**. Peel the backing off **16** and iron into position on **17**. Peel the backing off **17** and iron into position on the background (piece **28**). Zigzag stitch in contrast coloured thread all around pieces **15**, **16** and **17**.

3 Pin the pocket pieces into position and beginning at point A with a bar tack, stitch close to the edge of the pocket around to point B. End with another bar tack. Repeat with the other pocket.

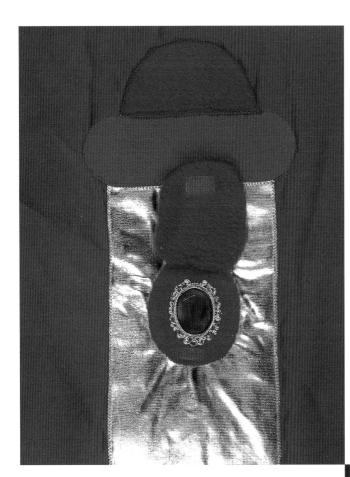

Making the funnels

1 Trace the shapes of **18**, **19**, **20**, **21**, **22** and **23** onto the paper side of fusible webbing. Cut them out roughly and iron **18** and **19** onto the back of silver fabric, **20** and **21** onto blue fun fur fabric, and **22** and **23** onto pink fun fur fabric. Cut them out neatly. Peel off the backing paper and iron them into position on the background and zigzag stitch all around the edges in contrast thread.

2 Cut out the oval shape of **24** and **25** from your newspaper drawing. Use it as a template to cut out two ovals of pink fun fur. Pin **25** into position in the centre of **19** with the squeaker underneath. Stitch all around the edge with a zigzag stitch. Pin **24** in position in the centre of **18** and zigzag stitch all around the edge to hold.

3 Handsew the mirror securely to the centre of **24**. Cut a little strip of the hooked side of Velcro and stitch it to the fun fur under the mirror.

4 Cut another two ovals out of pink fun fur, this time adding a 1cm (½in) seam allowance all the way round. These are the lid pieces **26** and **27**. Stitch the soft side of the Velcro strip to the right side of **26**. With right sides together, pin **26** and **27** together and, leaving a 1cm (½in) seam allowance, stitch around the edge, leaving a 4cm (1¾in) gap between the beginning and end of your stitching. Turn the lid right way out, turn in the raw edges across the gap and stitch to the top of **24**.

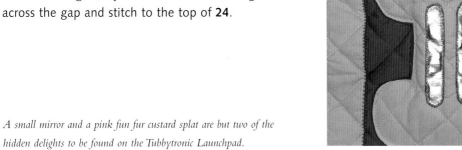

A small mirror and a pink fun fur custard splat are but two of the hidden delights to be found on the Tubbytronic Launchpad.

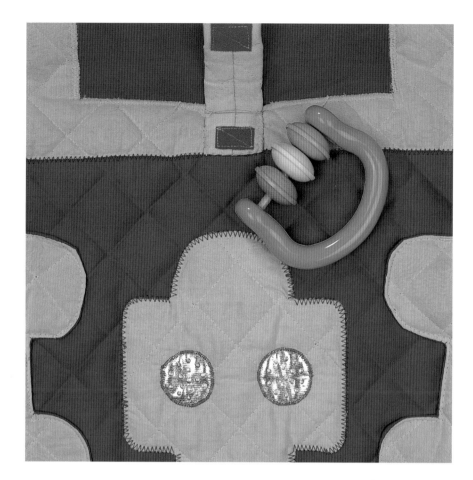

Finishing off

1 Turn the whole work wrong side up and lay a piece of polyester wadding on top. Cut wadding to fit and baste to playmat (**28**) around all sides. Turn playmat right side up, and lay the corduroy piece (**34**) face down on top. Taking a 1.5cm (⅝in) seam allowance, stitch **28** and **34** together around all sides, leaving a 30cm (12in) opening on one side.

2 Turn the whole playmat right side out through this opening, and then stitch up the opening by hand. Finally, apply dots of pearlised silver fabric paint to circles **13** and **14** to create a texture. Leave to dry for 24 hours.

The rattle (left) can be easily removed to be played with and then re-attached to prevent loss; Dipsy's hat (below) remains attached at all times but its texture is very comforting.

Adding the extra delights

1 Cut a strip (**29**) 10 x 8cm (4 x 3½in) of pink quilted polycotton. With right sides together, fold it in half lengthways and, leaving a 1cm (½in) seam allowance, stitch together along the longer edge. Turn the tube right side out, press the seam, tuck in the raw ends and stitch a hooked and a soft piece of Velcro to either end. Stitch **29** in place at the centre top of **17**. Use this to attach the hand-held rattle.

2 Cut pieces **30** and **31** out of pink fun fur for the custard splat. With right sides together, pin **30** and **31** together and, leaving a 1cm (½in) seam allowance, stitch around the edge, leaving a 4cm (1¾in) gap between the beginning and end of your stitching. Turn the splat right sides out through the gap and stuff it with a piece of screwed up cellophane. Stitch up the gap by hand, attaching one end of a piece of tape securely into the seam as you do. Attach the other end of the tape to the underside of pocket **11**.

3 Cut pieces **32** and **33** out of black and white cow fun fur for Dipsy's hat. Make a rattle to go inside by putting a couple of dried beans into the empty Tic-tac box and tape the lid securely shut with a piece of packaging tape. Make up the hat as for the custard splat above, inserting the rattle instead of the cellophane. Stitch the tape end to the underside of pocket **12**.

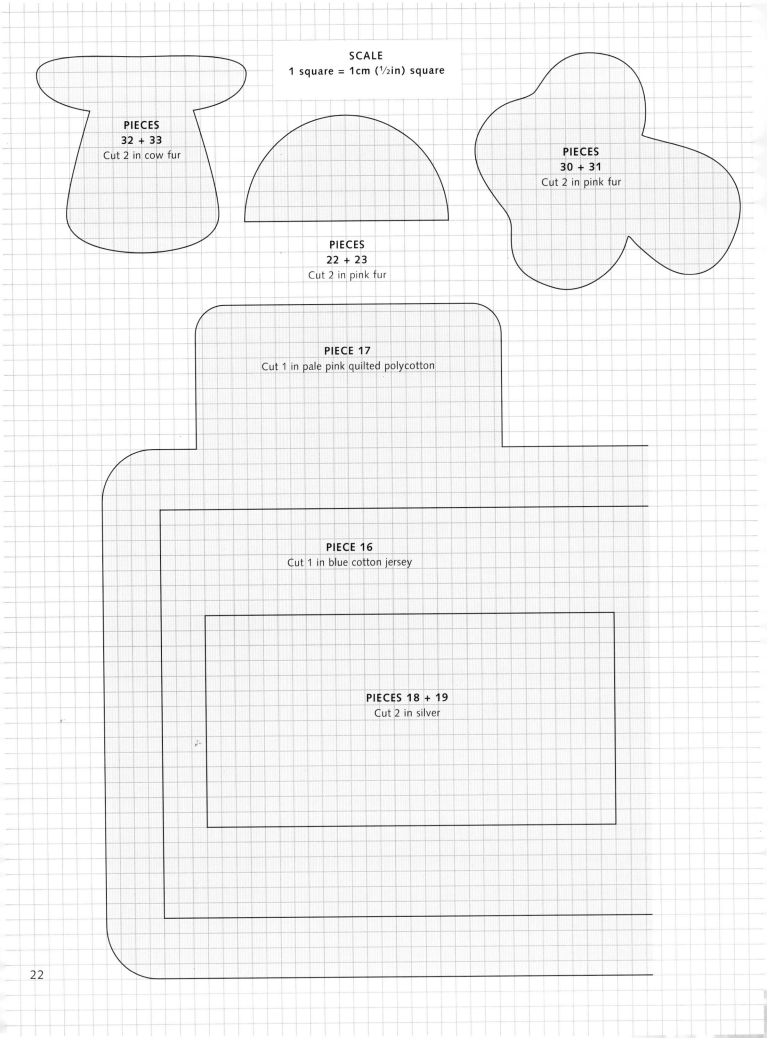

SCALE
1 square = 1cm (½in) square

PIECES
32 + 33
Cut 2 in cow fur

PIECES
22 + 23
Cut 2 in pink fur

PIECES
30 + 31
Cut 2 in pink fur

PIECE 17
Cut 1 in pale pink quilted polycotton

PIECE 16
Cut 1 in blue cotton jersey

PIECES 18 + 19
Cut 2 in silver

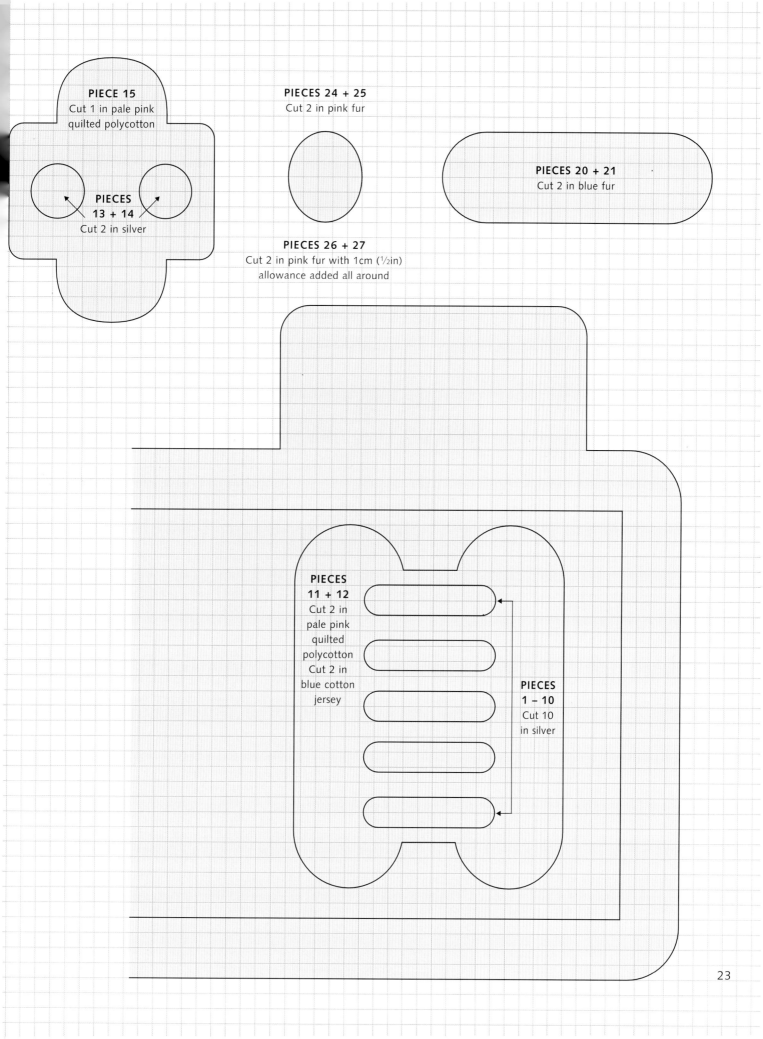

PIECE 15
Cut 1 in pale pink
quilted polycotton

PIECES 24 + 25
Cut 2 in pink fur

PIECES 20 + 21
Cut 2 in blue fur

**PIECES
13 + 14**
Cut 2 in silver

PIECES 26 + 27
Cut 2 in pink fur with 1cm (½in)
allowance added all around

**PIECES
11 + 12**
Cut 2 in
pale pink
quilted
polycotton
Cut 2 in
blue cotton
jersey

**PIECES
1 – 10**
Cut 10
in silver

The Sun Photoframe

THE WONDERFUL THING about salt dough is that you will probably have all the ingredients for the dough in your kitchen cupboard right now, and could start this project without further ado! However, it takes in the region of 6 hours to bake and it should go in the oven as soon as it's ready as the dough is more likely to crack if it has been waiting around and has dried out too much. In other words, don't mix up your dough just before you need the oven for baking, or too late in the evening, or you may find yourself having to sit up into the early hours of the morning.

You will have quite a lot of dough left over after you've made the frame, but children will be only too willing to help you use up the rest for making Christmas decorations, Valentine hearts, Easter baskets or even a Teletubby or two.

MATERIALS
- *salt dough (see recipe below)*
- *paper clip*
- *rolling pin*
- *flat baking tray at least 30cm (12in) square*
- *acrylic paints in yellow, white and red*
- *clear acrylic or polyurethane varnish*
- *close-up photograph of your baby enlarged or photocopied to the right size*
- *cardboard*
- *adhesive*
- *double-sided tape*
- *felt (optional)*

Making the salt dough frame

1 Collect the following ingredients to make up the dough:

- *280g (10oz/2 level cups) plain flour*
- *310g (11oz/1 level cup) cooking salt*
- *180ml (¾ cup) water*
- *10ml (2tsp) cooking oil*

Mix together the flour and salt and then add the water and oil. Continue mixing until they are bound together (adding a tiny bit more water if necessary) and then turn out onto an unfloured work surface and knead for at least ten minutes until the dough is smooth, pliable and slightly tacky. Check it by rolling a piece into a small ball – it shouldn't crack. When it is ready, roll out the dough to a thickness of about 1cm (½in).

2 Enlarge the outline of the baby sun overleaf on a photocopier to the size you require. (Ours was enlarged until the diameter of the centre was 9cm [3½in].) Cut it out, including the circle in the centre, and lay it on top of the rolled-out dough. Cut around the sun and the central circle with a non-serrated kitchen knife. Smooth round the edges with a finger dipped in water. Then lift one of the sun's rays and stick a paper clip into the dough to make a hanging loop.

3 Place the sun on a greased baking tray and bake in the oven at 130°C (265°F/Gas Mark 1) for 5 – 6 hours. Check it after about 4 hours, and when the top is baked solid, slide it off the baking tray and on to a cooling rack and put back in the oven to continue hardening underneath. When the dough is hard on both sides, turn off the heat and leave the frame in the oven to cool off gradually.

Decorating the frame

1 Now for the painting. Paint the whole frame yellow, remembering to cover all the outside edges and inside of the circle. Mix a bit of red into some yellow paint and paint quick and free brush strokes of warm orange radiating from the centre. Finish by mixing white with yellow and add some paler yellow highlights in the centre. Acrylic paint is very easy to use and is water-soluble. If you are inexperienced and nervous try it out on your photocopied template first. And if you really make a mess of it, let it dry for about half an hour and then paint over your failed attempt with another yellow base coat and try again.

2 When the paint is dry, cover the whole frame – front and back and every nook and cranny – with two coats of clear varnish. This seals the dough so it is important to cover every surface completely.

3 Enlarge the photograph so that the baby's head fills the centre hole of the frame. Stick the photograph onto cardboard, trim to size, and then stick to the back of the frame with double-sided tape. For extra protection, you can finish off the back of the frame with a piece of felt.

Tubby Toast and Custard Splat Fridge Magnets

YOU CAN BUY plastic modelling clay that hardens in a domestic oven at most art and craft shops. It is harder to work than other clays but these simple custard splat and toast shapes shouldn't present a problem even if you haven't modelled anything since your childhood. The advantage is that, once baked, it is very light which is important if the magnet is going to have enough strength to hold up your child's artwork and survive the constant jolting as the fridge door is opened and closed. For the same reason, buy the strongest magnets you can find.

A word of caution: the chemicals used in this kind of modelling clay are toxic before and during the hardening process. Don't use it with very young children around, and if older children want to be involved with making these magnets, explain to them first not to put either the clay or their fingers in their mouths and to wash their hands thoroughly after use. Also, keep a window open in the kitchen during baking and make sure that any household implements used for the modelling are washed well afterwards.

MATERIALS
- *plastic modelling clay in bright pink and brown*
- *rolling pin*
- *skewer or used ball-point pen*
- *craft knife or non-serrated kitchen knife*
- *baking tray*
- *packet of magnets*
- *high-impact adhesive*
- *acrylic paint in white*

Working with modelling clay

1. Break off a small piece of modelling clay and warm it up by kneading and rolling it in the palm of your hand to make it more pliable.

2. With a rolling pin, roll it out on a flat surface to a thickness of about 3mm (⅛in).

27

Making the magnets

1 For the custard splats, use a skewer or ball-point pen which has run out of ink to draw the custard splat shapes (see the template to the right) onto the bright pink clay. Cut around these shapes with a craft knife or the blade of a non-serrated edge kitchen knife. Round off the edges by smoothing round the shapes with your fingers.

2 For the toast, choose a round implement to use as a cutter. We used the screw top from a small jam jar. Cut two circles from the brown clay, and roll one out a bit more for the larger bottom circle. In the smaller circle cut out two eyes and a mouth. When you are happy with your face, put this circle on top of the larger one.

3 Bake the shapes on a baking tray in the middle of the oven at 130°C (265°F/Gas Mark 1) for 25 minutes.

4 When the shapes have cooled, use a dab of high-impact glue to fix the magnets to the back. Remember to check which way round to use the magnets – if you glue it on the wrong way it will repel rather then attach itself to metal! Finally, use small quantities of white acrylic paint to highlight the eyes and mouth on the tubby toast magnets.

Tubby Toast Countdown Calendar

WHENEVER THERE IS an exciting event coming up, whether it be birthday, holiday or the first day of term, use this Tubby Toast Countdown Calendar to help the week of suspense on its way. Everyday another button can be pulled out of the toaster to reveal a removable sticker that your child can stick on a shirt or in a scrapbook. On the final day, the toast at the top of the machine can be pulled out to reveal a big sticker and perhaps the words: 'Hooray! It's today!'. If you use reusable adhesive to attach the stickers, you will be able to replace them and use the calendar 'Again, again'!

Making the toaster

MATERIALS
- *1cm (¹/₂in) squared paper*
- *silver card*
- *highlighter pen in pale blue*
- *craft knife*
- *blue and pink metallic card (or sweet wrappers, ironed out and stuck flat onto card)*
- *brown paper (or a large brown envelope)*
- *small piece of white paper*
- *pack of Teletubby glitter stickers (or you can make your own by drawing Teletubby motifs onto sticky labels)*
- *sticky pads*
- *reusable adhesive*
- *art and craft spray adhesive*

1 Enlarge the templates overleaf to an appropriate size (ours is 30cm [15in] wide and 44cm [22in] tall) (see page 112). Transfer the outline of the tubby toast machine onto the back of the silver card and cut it out. Then use the highlighter pen to draw the blue decoration on the front of the toast machine. Make a vertical slot 5cm (2½in) long – preferably with a craft knife – in the side where the No.1 button will slide in.

2 Cut the No.1 tab from silver card. Then cut the No.1 button from blue card and stick it to one end of the tab with double-sided tape. Write 1 on the front and attach a sticker to the other end of the tab with a tiny piece of reusable adhesive so that it can be removed and replaced easily. Slide the tab into the slot on the toaster.

3 Cut a piece of card 8 x 4cm (4 x 2in) and stick a sticky pad to either end. Turn the toaster face down and stick this piece of card onto the back so that it acts as a runner guide for the No.1 tab.

4 Using the templates overleaf, cut the No.7 tab and button as one piece out of silver card. Also cut two brown paper circles for the toast. Make one of them slightly smaller than the other. On the back of the smaller one draw eyes and a mouth in pencil. Cut them out and then stick a small sheet of white paper behind them. Stick the two brown paper circles together and then stick them to the No.7 button. Write 7 at the top of the toast. Attach a sticker to the bottom of the lollipop shape with reusable adhesive and write 'Hooray! It's Today!' above it.

5 Cut a piece of card 10 x 4cm (5 x 2in) and stick a sticky pad to either end. Turn the toaster face down and position the toast so that only the top edge will show from the front. Stick down the piece of card so that the toast will rest in it at the right height.

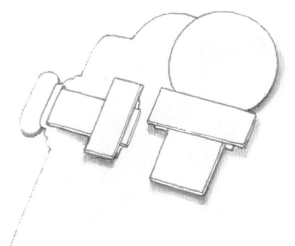

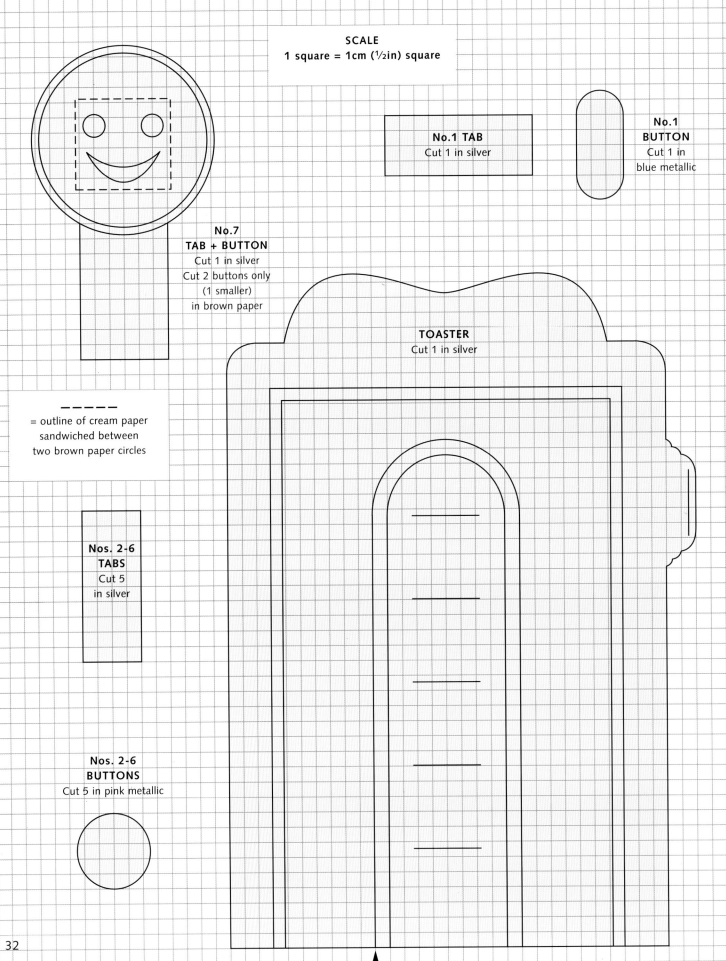

SCALE
1 square = 1cm (½in) square

No.1 TAB
Cut 1 in silver

No.1 BUTTON
Cut 1 in blue metallic

No.7 TAB + BUTTON
Cut 1 in silver
Cut 2 buttons only
(1 smaller)
in brown paper

= outline of cream paper
sandwiched between
two brown paper circles

TOASTER
Cut 1 in silver

Nos. 2-6 TABS
Cut 5 in silver

Nos. 2-6 BUTTONS
Cut 5 in pink metallic

Cutting line for CENTRE PANEL

The finishing touches

1. Cut the centre panel of the toaster out of silver card. Make five evenly spaced horizontal slots each 5cm (2½in) wide as marked on the template opposite. Stick the centre panel to the toaster with sticky pads.

2. Cut five Nos. 2–6 tabs out of silver card and five Nos. 2–6 buttons out of pink card and number them 2 to 6. Using double-sided tape stick one end of each silver tab to the centre of each circle. Attach a sticker to the other end of the tab and slide them into the slots on the centre panel of the toaster. Add the blue edging around the centre panel with the highlighter pen.

Tubby Dice Stool

YOU CAN THROW and roll this dice, count the Teletubby images on each face and use it as a stool. You can also make up lots of games to play with it. Try this one: agree a set of actions for each face of the dice. For instance, when the toast face is uppermost, act out eating tubby toast. Picking flowers, slurping tubby custard, touching the clouds, hiding like a Teletubby behind a hill and going to sleep in the Tubbytronic Superdome could be actions for the other faces. Roll the dice and start acting!

The pictures on each face have been painted with fabric pens. These come in wonderful bright colours but you might need to practise before decorating fabric with them. Use them terribly lightly as the colour will bleed into the fabric if you hold the pen still for too long. Iron your work between applications of each colour to fix the paint and stop colours bleeding into each other.

MATERIALS
- *fusible webbing*
- *50cm (½yd) lightweight cotton in white*
- *fabric pens in red, yellow, green, purple, blue, pink, black and brown*
- *50cm (½yd) furnishing weight cotton in pink, blue and green*
- *sewing machine*
- *contrast coloured sewing thread*
- *30cm (12in) cube of firm fire-retardant foam*
- *embroidery cotton in yellow*

Making the appliqué squares

1. Draw 21 squares each measuring 7cm (2¾in) square on the paper side of the fusible webbing. Trace the pictures on pages 36–8 onto each square in pencil: 1 x dome, 2 x clouds, 3 x tubby toasts, 4 x Teletubbies (note that on page 37 four different templates are provided), 5 x flowers, 6 x custard splats. Iron the fusible webbing onto the back of the white cotton.

2. Turn the cotton right side up and you should be able to see your traced drawings through the cotton. Using the fabric pens, colour in each picture. Cut out all the squares.

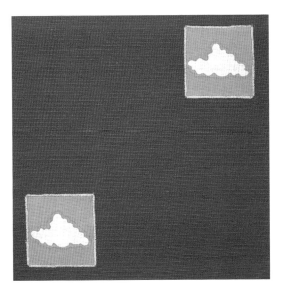

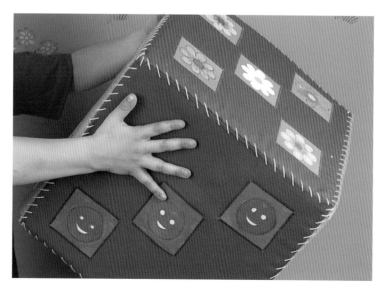

Making the cube

1 Cut 2 squares each measuring 33cm (13in) square in each of the three colours of furnishing weight cotton. Peel the paper backing off all the picture squares and position them on the big squares. You can do this by eye. Bond each picture square into position by pressing with a medium iron for at least 15 seconds.

2 With the width setting at medium on your sewing machine, work satin stitch around each square in bright contrast cotton.

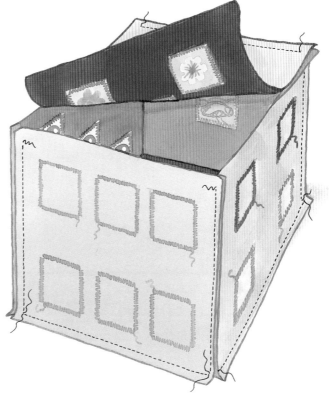

3 Now sew together all the squares with right sides together. Using the layout here as a guide, start by sewing side 4 to side 2. Next sew 6 to 2, 3 to 2 and then 1 to 2. Then stitch 1 to 4, 4 to 6, 6 to 3 and 3 to 1 and lastly, stitch 5 to 1, leaving three sides of the last square unstitched. Turn the fabric right side out and insert the foam. Sew up the last sides by hand.

4 With bright yellow embroidery cotton and using all six strands of thread together, oversew all the edges of the dice with large slanting stitches.

To ensure you sew the faces together in the correct order, lay out the squares as here.

Tubbytronic Superdome Cake

YOU'LL NEVER BUY a shop-bought birthday cake once you realise how easy it is to make your own delightful cake in the shape of the Tubbytronic Superdome. To make things simple we've suggested using a packet cake mix, but if you'd rather use your own recipe, feel free. Make the cake the day before you're going to ice it as it is easier then to cut and decorate. Make the Teletubbies and windows at the same time because this takes some time and they need to dry a little before being handled. For best results make butter icing on the day it is to be used and do not refrigerate. If it has to be left for any length of time before icing the cake, keep it covered or it will develop a crust.

MATERIALS

- *plain sponge cake mix, plus eggs, water, oil or milk as specified on the packet*
- *2 x 20cm (8in) round cake tins, lightly greased*
- *28cm (11in) cake board or a round bread board covered with kitchen foil*
- *jam*
- *small packet of white roll-out icing*
- *packet of mixed coloured roll-out icing*
- *liquid food colouring in black, blue and green*
- *paint brush (fine)*
- *1 packet each of the following cake decorations: silver balls, sugar flowers, hundreds and thousands, sugar confetti*
- *empty cereal packet or card*
- *tweezers*

Making the cake

1 Following the manufacturer's instructions, mix and bake the cake in the round cake tins. When cooked, remove the tins from the oven and let them stand for about 3 minutes before shaking the tins gently to make sure they are free from the base and sides.

2 Turn the cakes onto a wire rack, one dome-side up and one dome-side down, and leave to cool. When cool, put the flatter cake on the cake board, spread it with jam and put the domed cake on top.

Making the butter icing

1 Gather together the following ingredients:

- *100g (4oz) butter*
- *2 – 3 tsp milk*
- *200g (8oz) icing sugar, sifted*
- *a few drops of vanilla flavouring*
- *green food colouring*

2 Let the butter and milk get to room temperature. Beat the butter with an electric mixer (or a wooden spoon and some elbow grease) until it turns white.

3 Gradually add half the sifted icing sugar, beating all the time. Then slowly add the milk and vanilla and the rest of the icing sugar. Lastly, gradually add the food colouring. The mixture should be smooth and easy to spread with a spatula. If the colouring has made it too runny add some more icing sugar to the right consistency.

Making the windows

1 To make the windows fit the side of your cake, make a template out of card by drawing around a cup or mug and trimming off the bottom to the height of the edge of your cake.

2 Mix 75g (3oz) of white roll-out icing with two peas of black roll-out icing to make it grey. Roll it out gently on the grey side of a cereal packet because it is quite sticky and the dry and porous card will make it easier to roll. If necessary, sprinkle a little icing sugar onto your rolling pin.

3 When it is about 2mm ($\frac{1}{10}$in) thick, cut around the card template with a sharp knife to make four windows. Leave the shapes on the card to dry and save the rest of the grey icing to make the Teletubby tummies. Also keep the card template until the next day because you will need it when shaping the cake.

4 Trace the petal-shaped window panes below onto a piece of paper and cut out around the edge and the panes. When the icing windows have dried a bit, lay the paper template on top and, using the fine paintbrush and black food colouring, paint in the window panes. Leave to dry.

5 At the same time as you are making the windows, use the black roll-out icing in the coloured packet to make a 3.5cm (1$\frac{1}{3}$in) diameter circle for the hole at the top of the dome. Leave to dry with the windows.

Making the Teletubbies

1 For Dipsy and Laa-Laa use the green and yellow roll-out icing straight from the coloured packet. For Po, mix 20g (1oz) red icing with 10g ($\frac{1}{2}$oz) white and add a drop of blue food colouring. For Tinky Winky, mix 20g (1oz) white with 10g ($\frac{1}{2}$oz) red and add several drops of blue food colouring.

2 Knead and roll a golf ball size (30g [1oz]) of the appropriately coloured roll-out icing into an oval shape. Make cuts in the oval for the arms and legs. Pull the arms and legs out and shape them using your fingers and the end of a paint brush. Press in around the eye areas with your fingers, and pinch out the ears. Sit the figure down on card and make a hole in the top of its head with the end of a paint brush or a cocktail stick.

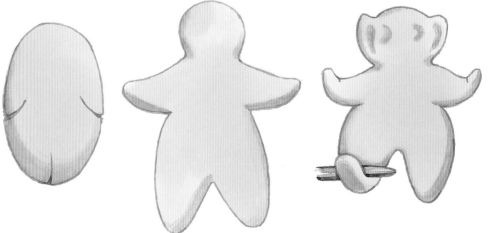

3 Use a bit of leftover grey window icing rolled out very thinly to cut four square tummy screens for the Teletubbies' tummies. Stick into position using water brushed on as glue.

4 For the faces, mix a small marble of white roll-out icing with a small marble of green and a quarter marble of red to get a flesh tone. For Dipsy's face, add a tiny amount of black icing. Divide it in four and roll each out thinly to make a circle. Glue onto the front of each Teletubby head with water and use the end of a paint brush to make eyes and a mouth. Use tiny off-cuts of the flesh coloured icing to make ears and glue them into position.

5 Roll out a thin sausage of icing for each aerial in the appropriate colours. Twist them into the correct shapes and leave to dry for a while. When they are stiff enough, stick them into the hole on the top of each head and stick into place with a little water.

Icing and decorating the cake

1 Slice four flat sides off the cake the width of the card window template.

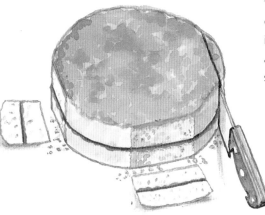

2 Hold the template against each side in turn and, using a sharp knife, cut the sponge away around the window about 2.5cm (1in) deep at the top and less near the bottom. Shape the dome by cutting the sponge from the top edge, leaving the windows intact.

3 Coat the cake and board with green butter icing (see recipe on page 40). Press the window shapes onto the flat sides cut on the cake. Spread butter icing over the edge of the windows and use tweezers to apply the silver balls around the windows.

4 Put sugar flowers between the windows and sprinkle hundreds and thousands around them. Separate some flower shapes from the sugar confetti and use tweezers to drop into the flower arrangements.

5 Press the black circle on to the top of the cake and sit the Teletubbies around it. Do all this immediately after the cake has been iced as it will crust over after a while. Finally, wipe around the edge of the board to clean it up.

Teletubbyland

Teletubby Snuggledown

THIS CRISP WHITE BEDLINEN set of a single quilt cover and two pillowcases is made of practical easycare polycotton. The appliquéd and embroidered Teletubby borders are made separately and then applied to the main fabric so that you don't have to manoeuvre vast swathes of fabric about the sewing machine. If you haven't done a lot of this kind of work, all it takes is a little practice. Have a go at making a couple of spare appliqués before you start the real thing, following the tips overleaf. When you've built up confidence, proceed with the real thing.

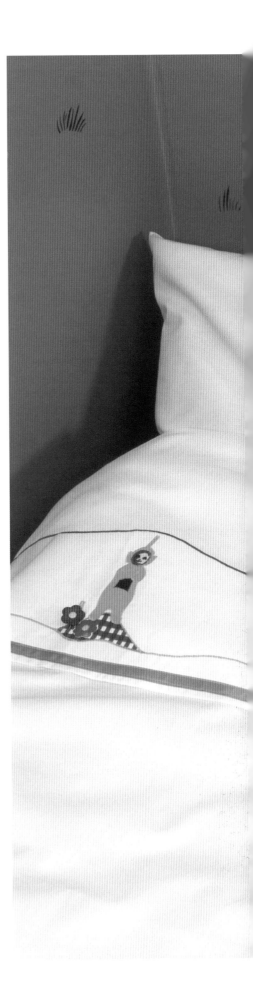

MATERIALS

- *1.5m (1½yd) of 46cm (18in) wide fusible webbing*
- *sewing machine with a zigzag facility*
- *6.5m (7yd) white polycotton 137cm (54in) wide or 4.25m (4¾yd) white polycotton sheeting 230cm (90in) wide cut as follows:*
- **Quilt:** *1 piece measuring 137 x 423cm (4ft 6in x 13ft 10in)*
- **Pillowcases:** *2 pieces, each measuring 50 x 168cm (20in x 5ft 6in)*
- **Appliquéd borders:** *1 strip measuring 137 x 15cm (4ft 6in x 6in) and 2 strips, each measuring 50 x 15cm (20 x 6in)*
- *10cm (4in) of polycotton in red, lime green, bright yellow, purple, cream and grey*
- *10cm (4in) patterned polycotton*
- *small, sharp scissors*
- *tailor's chalk*
- *sewing thread in red, lime green, yellow, purple, cream and blue*
- *embroidery silks in red, lime green, yellow, purple and brown*
- *2.5m (2¾yd) of 1cm (½in) wide satin ribbon in lime green*
- *7 flower-shaped buttons in various colours*

Preparing the appliqué

1 Trace two of each Teletubby template from pages 113–116 onto the smooth side of the fusible webbing. Trace the faces and tummy screens separately and identify each one in the middle of the tracings so that you don't get muddled later. Trace 8 hill shapes from below (4 for the quilt and 2 for each pillowcase). Cut roughly round all the templates.

2 Iron the fusible webbing with the Teletubby tracings onto the appropriately coloured polycotton. Iron all the faces onto the cream polycotton and all the tummy screens onto the grey polycotton. Iron the hill shapes onto the patterned polycotton. Cut them all out carefully with small sharp scissors.

3 Decide how you are going to space the appliqués on the border strips. Then peel the paper backing off the patterned hill shapes and iron them into position, following the manufacturer's instructions carefully. With tailor's chalk, draw a wavy line right across the bottom of the border linking each hill. Machine along this line and around each hill with lime green satin stitch with a medium stitch width.

4 Peel the paper backing off each Teletubby and iron them into position on each hill. Satin stitch around each one in the appropriate coloured thread. This takes care and practice – see the tips box above for advice.

SEWING HINTS AND TIPS

- Set your machine to a slower setting if you have one.
- If possible, use a perspex presser foot so that you can see what you are doing.
- Keep the centre mark of the presser foot just inside the raw edge of the appliqué.
- When stitching around the difficult bits like ears and aerials, stop the machine with the needle still in the work, lift the presser foot and turn the work manually. Do this every few stitches if necessary.
- Don't worry if it doesn't look machine-made perfect. It won't, because after all you are not a machine and it all adds to the charm in the end.

5 Peel the paper backing off each face and tummy screen and iron them into position on each Teletubby. Satin stitch around the tummy screen with the colour of whichever Teletubby it is on. Satin stitch around each face with cream or brown cotton. Satin stitch some cream or brown into each ear.

6 Embroider the eyes, nose and mouth onto each face by hand. It helps to draw the outline of the features in very light pencil first. Embroider the Teletubbies' names onto the pillowcase borders in the appropriate colours with simple hand backstitching.

Applying the borders

1 Cut fusible webbing the same size as the borders and iron on to the back of each border. Draw a wavy line onto the paper side of the fusible webbing along the top of the quilt border and along both left-hand sides of the pillowcase borders (right-hand side if you're looking at them from the back). Cut along the wavy lines.

2 At one end of the quilt fabric make a hem by pressing over 1.5cm (½in) to the right side (there won't be a right or wrong side to unprinted polycotton, so you decide which it is). Peel the paper backing off the quilt border and lay it down on the main fabric so that the bottom raw edge of the border meets the hem. Iron the border down. Repeat this step with each pillowcase piece.

3 Thread your machine with blue cotton and carefully work satin stitch along the wavy edges of the quilt and pillowcase borders.

The Buttons

FOR THE BUTTONS on the quilt we found some intriguing two-part daisy buttons where the centre pops out so we were able to swap the colours around to make the great two-tone combinations. They are made of white nylon which we coloured with hot water dye. The whole process is incredibly quick and easy because as soon as the buttons are plunged into the simmering saucepan of dye on the hob the nylon soaks up the dye.

Before starting, cover your kitchen surface with newspaper to protect against dye splashes and wear rubber gloves. Also have a sieve or slotted spoon and a bowl of cold water ready. Scoop out the buttons to check on the colour, and when you are happy with the shade reached, plunge them in the water. The colour continues to get deeper, even when out of the dye so it is better to fish them out looking too pale rather than too dark. You can always put them back in again later if you think they need it.

The finishing touches

1 Pin the lime green satin ribbon over the straight raw edge of each border. Stitch close to both sides of the ribbon with two rows of straight stitch. Make sure that the ribbon is parallel to the folded edge of the main fabric as you stitch.

2 Decide where you are going to position the buttons on the quilt. We made sure that each buttonhole 'grew' out of the wavy green satin stitching which meant that they were at slightly different heights all the way along. Make the buttonholes with lime green thread to match.

49

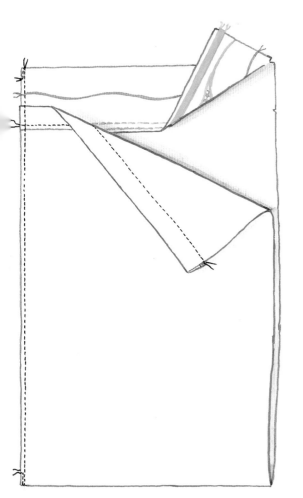

Making up the quilt

1 At the other end of the fabric from the border make a 10cm (4in) hem by folding in to the wrong side first 1.5cm (⅝in) and then 10cm (4in). Press and pin. Stitch in place close to the inside folded edge.

2 Lay the quilt fabric on a flat surface right side up. Make notches in both side seam allowances 30cm (12in) and 50cm (20in) down from the border edge. Take the border end and fold it at the 30cm (12in) marks. Then take the opposite end and fold it so that the edge meets the two 50cm (20in) marks (and overlaps the border by 10cm [4in]). Pin along both side seams.

3 Leaving a 1.5cm (⅝in) seam allowance, stitch down both side seams, backstitching at the beginning and end of each seam. Turn the quilt cover right side out.

4 With a stitch ripper or small sharp scissors, carefully cut open all the buttonholes. To mark the positions where the buttons are to be sewn to the fabric beneath, poke a pencil through the buttonholes. Sew on all the buttons with strong cotton.

Making up the pillowcases

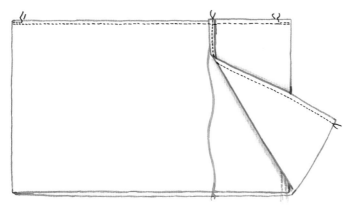

1 At the end of the fabric opposite the border, make a 12mm (½in) double hem on the wrong side of the fabric and stitch in place close to the inside folded edge. Fold this edge 15cm (6in) to the right side and press.

2 Open out the fold and turn the pillowcase right side up. Take the bordered end and fold so that it is aligned with the crease. Fold the hemmed end along the creaseline over the bordered end. Pin and baste both side seams.

3 Leaving a 1.5cm (⅝in) seam allowance, machine the side seams, backstitching at the beginning and end of each seam. Turn the pillowcase right side out. Repeat for the other pillowcase.

Tubby Bye-byes

CHOOSING THE RIGHT time to move your child out of a cot and into a real bed can be tricky. But with some forethought and preparation you can smooth the transition. With this bedhead cover you will be able to create lots of bedtime rituals to make the end of the day a time to look forward to for both you and your child. Move the sun into its cloud pocket, and say 'tele bye-bye' to each tiny felt Teletubby as you pop them into the big pocket behind the hills. Your child will find lots more room in the pockets to store favourite books and soft toys as well.

MATERIALS

- *1.5m (1½yd) sky blue fabric (or twice the height of the bed head)*
- *1.25m (1¼yd) grass green fabric*
- *tailor's chalk or pencil*
- *1 square each of lime green, purple, red, yellow, white, brown and orange felt; plus scraps of cerise, forest green, lilac, sky blue, black, grey and beige felt*
- *pinking shears*
- *sharp embroidery scissors*
- *embroidery threads in yellow, pink and dark brown*
- *7 Velcro spots*
- *fusible webbing*
- *polyester filling, kapok or cotton wool*
- *2.5m (2¾yd) gingham ribbon for ties*

Cutting the cover

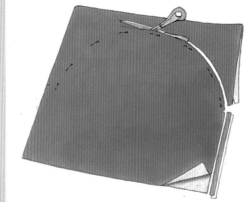

1 Cut two pieces of blue fabric to the shape of the bed head plus 5cm (2in) seam allowances. To do this, fold the fabric over the bed head. Allowing at least 5cm (2in) seam allowances, pin around the fabric to fit. It needs to be loose enough to slip on and off.

2 Mark the start of the side slits for maximum ease of removal by cutting a notch in the seam allowance. Take the cover off the bed head with the pins still in and trim the seam allowance to 2cm (¾in). Remove the pins, leaving two pieces of fabric.

Adding the hills

1 Fold the green fabric in half with right sides together and lay it on top of the front piece of the blue cover. Cut the green layers to fit the lower two-thirds of the cover. Draw in the three hill shapes along the top in tailor's chalk. With right sides facing, machine the two pieces of fabric together along the chalk line.

2 Trim the excess fabric above to within 12mm (½in) of the stitch line and snip into the seam allowance at 2.5cm (1in) intervals. Turn the fabric right sides out and press. Top stitch very close to the seam edge.

3 Continue drawing the line of the hills towards the centre of the cover with the tailor's chalk. Then satin stitch over the chalk line, starting at the top with the widest stitch setting and decreasing the width so that the line tapers off towards the bottom.

4 Using pinking shears and the lime green, purple, red, yellow, cerise, forest green, lilac and sky blue felts, cut out three five-petalled flower heads and two circles from each colour. Cut 40 tiny black triangles.

5 Stitch a triangle to the centre of each shape with a French knot in yellow embroidery thread (see below) and then stitch each flower onto the hillsides. Intersperse the flowers with 6 Velcro spots (the hooked sides), decoratively stitched on with coloured embroidery threads.

6 Pin the green hills onto the blue front piece. Machine stitch all layers together across the width where the top of the mattress meets the bed head. The pocket then isn't bottomless.

Adding the decorative details

1 Using the template on page 117, trace the windmill outline onto the paper side of the fusible webbing, cut out, peel off the backing and iron it onto grey felt and cut out. Position the windmill at the top of the centre hill on the blue background, peel off the backing and iron in place. Machine stitch close to the edge all around the windmill and embroider stars in pink embroidery thread. Stitch the top of the centre hill to the blue background just beneath the windmill so that the pocket won't flop forwards.

2 Using the template on page 117, cut one large cloud in white felt. Pin the cloud onto the blue background and stitch into place as for the windmill.

3 Cut out one smaller cloud in white felt and stitch the hooked side of a Velcro spot into the centre. Stitch the cloud (behind the sun in the picture on page 53) onto the blue background.

Finishing the cover

1 Pin the back to the front with right sides facing and, leaving a 2cm (³/₄in) seam allowance, machine stitch between the notches at the top of the side slits. Trim the seam to 12mm (¹/₂in) and snip at 2.5cm (1in) intervals along the curved seam.

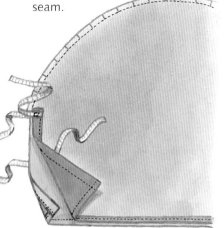

2 Using the curved end of an ironing board, mould the curved seam, pressing it open. To neaten the raw edges along the front and back of each side slit opening, fold in a double hem, press and machine stitch. Repeat with the bottom edge of the front and back covers.

3 Cut the gingham ribbon into eight 30cm (12in) lengths. Pin each ribbon into position on the front and back of each side slit (two pairs on each slit) and hand stitch securely.

Making the extras

1 Using the templates on pages 113–116 and appropriate colours of felt, cut out two pieces for each Teletubby. Stitch the soft side of a Velcro spot onto the back piece of each. Trace four face shapes and four TV screen shapes onto the paper side of fusible webbing. Iron the faces onto beige felt and the TV screens onto grey felt. Cut them out, remove the backing paper and iron into position on the front pieces.

2 Embroider the eyes and mouths with dark brown embroidery thread. Stitch together each pair of the bodies 5mm (¹/₄in) in from the edge, leaving an opening to insert the polyester filling. Stuff the bodies loosely and stitch up the openings. Trim carefully all around the edges, close to the stitching.

3 Cut out two pieces each for the sun (see the detail on page 52) and the two rabbits (see page 117) from felt scraps. Stitch the soft side of a Velcro spot onto the back piece of each. Make each one up and stuff as above.

Tubbytronic Window Blind

THIS IS A PROJECT that will transform a boring white roller blind into a window onto Teletubbyland. When it is dark outside, the silver background and the pearlised and glitter paints used to represent the lights inside the Superdome glisten and wink. In daylight, with the light coming from behind the blind, the view of hills and sky beyond the window comes to life. Don't use a blackout blind, though, because then the light won't shine through.

The stencilled image of the window is made with spray paints that come in lots of colours from any car accessory store. You must use them in very well-ventilated conditions, if not outdoors: a garage with the door wide open is probably the best place.

MATERIALS
- *squared paper*
- *newspaper*
- *low-tack masking tape*
- *long ruler*
- *string*
- *dinner plate*
- *saucer*
- *roller blind to fit the dimensions of your window*
- *art and craft spray adhesive*
- *2 screw-in hooks*
- *length of dowelling longer than the width of the blind*
- *decorator's mask*
- *large can of silver hubcap spray paint*
- *small cans of spray paint in green, pale blue and gunmetal*
- *fabric paints in silver pearlised and silver glitter*

Making the stencil

1 To make the blind stencil, transfer the scaled-down design overleaf onto squared paper, adjusting the proportions as necessary to fit your window.

2 Stick together sheets of newspaper with masking tape until you have a single sheet at least 10cm (4in) larger than the size of your design on each side. To make things more manageable on a large blind, divide the design into two parts – the petal-shaped window and then the round lights below.

3 Draw a line down the middle of the newspaper sheet to represent the centre of the blind. Draw a horizontal line at right angles in a position to represent the base of the window.

4 To draw the big semi-circle of the window work out the radius from your scale drawing. Then take a piece of string that is a longer than the radius and tie one end around your pencil. Hold the other end at exactly the length of the radius at the point where the two pencil lines cross. Hold the pencil upright and with the string taut, draw a semi-circle onto the newspaper.

5 Referring to your scale drawing, draw in the rest of the design. We used the dinner plate for the three big lights under the window, the cap of a spray can or an egg cup for the six lights inside and a saucer for the central round window pane and the ends of each petal.

6 Carefully cut out the petal shapes, the centre circle of the window and the big circles of the lights. Number the petal shapes as you go so that you don't muddle them up. You are going to need the background and the pieces you cut out as separate stencils so don't screw up anything.

Painting the blind

1 Prepare your spraying area very carefully as suggested to the right and temporarily hang up the blind (see right).

2 Draw a light pencil vertical line down the centre of the blind. You will have to use the big background stencil first to mark lightly in pencil the position of the petals and circles. Place it on the blind in the right position and fix with masking tape. Draw the cut-out shapes onto the blind. Remove the background stencil.

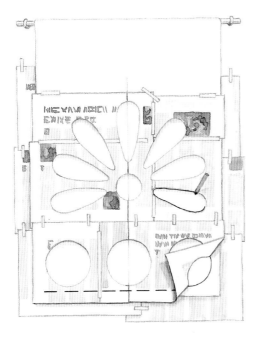

3 Lay the petal-shaped and circle stencils out flat on the floor and spray a light coat of art and craft spray adhesive over one at a time. Leave each to dry for a few seconds until it feels tacky and then stick onto the blind in the right position. Make sure the edges are stuck down so that the paint can't leak too far under the template.

Preparing for Spraying

- For ease of painting, hang the blind at a height where you don't have to squat too low to paint in the lights at the bottom but can still reach the top. Have a step ladder handy if you can't.
- Screw in the hooks slightly wider apart than the width of the blind. Insert the length of dowelling into the tube at the top end of the blind and rest it between the hooks.
- If there isn't a wind or through-draft in the room, the spray paint doesn't spread far but to prevent a silver outline on the wall, stick up sheets of newspaper with masking tape for protection. Put more on the floor where you are working.

4 Wearing the decorator's mask, carefully spray the whole blind with the silver paint. Move the can slowly and evenly back and forth across the blind. It will be patchy to start with but not for long. It is better to build up the silver background with several coats rather than hold the can in one position for too long – that will only create runs, which is not the desired effect.

5 Don't remove the stencils and leave the blind for about ten minutes to dry (and go somewhere else for some fresh air). Then draw in hill shapes on the stencils while they are still stuck to the blind. Remove them and cut in half along the hill outline. Number each half so that you don't muddle them up.

6 Turn the background of the window stencil face down on the floor and spray around the cut out shapes with spray adhesive and then stick it back in position on the blind with masking tape. Take the bottom half of the hill stencils and stick them in position (you might need to renew the spray adhesive). With the blue spray paint, lightly spray in the sky. Leave to dry for a few minutes.

7 Remove the hill stencils and replace with the sky stencils. With the green spray paint, lightly spray in the grass.

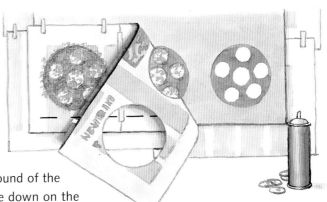

8 Turn the background of the lights stencil face down on the floor and spray around the cut-out shapes with spray adhesive and stick in position on the blind with masking tape. Cut the 3 bigger circles for the centre of each light, and 15 smaller circles out of some more newspaper and spray them with adhesive. Stick in the centre of each big circle on the blind. With the gunmetal spray paint, spray in the lights. Leave to dry as before and then remove all the stencils.

58

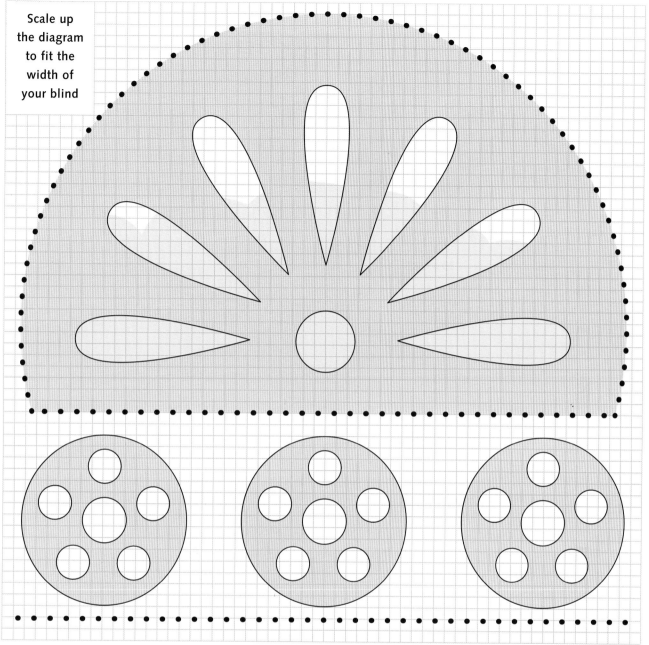

Scale up the diagram to fit the width of your blind

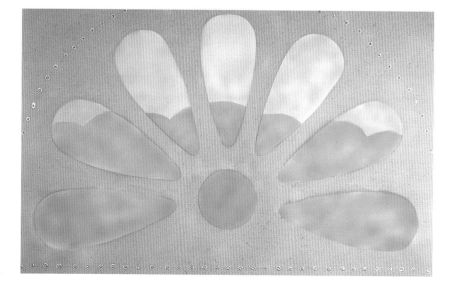

9 With the pearlised fabric paint draw a row of little circles along the bottom of the blind and all around the semi-circle of the window. Fill each circle with a blob of glitter paint. Leave the blind to dry for at least 24 hours and then follow the manufacturer's instructions for putting up the blind at your window.

59

Tubby Table Mat

THIS IS THE QUICKEST PROJECT in this book. All you need is a budding artist in the family and access to a good copy shop which offers a laminating service. The resulting table mat has a wipe-clean protective coating that will withstand hot plates and mugs (though not hot dishes and pans straight from the oven) and will help to encourage the fussiest toddler to eat up.

It doesn't have to be a work of art – if your child is younger, help by making a collage of Teletubby pictures that you have cut out of a magazine – 'sticking' is a highly rated activity among pre-schoolers. Or if you have a computer with access to the Internet you can download pictures for colouring in from the official BBC Teletubby Internet site (http://www.bbc.co.uk/education/teletubbies). Older children may consider themselves too old for a wipe-clean place mat, but they have better illustration skills and will be delighted to be commissioned to produce a drawing in consultation with and for a younger member of the family.

Take your child's Teletubby picture along to the copy shop and ask to have it enlarged to A3 size (11½ x 16½in). Trim off the white edges of the copy and then ask for it to be laminated in the thickest grade of lamination available. And that really is all there is to it!

Table mats like these would be perfect for a child's birthday party. Not only can they be used at the tea table but they make an excellent going-home present too.

Follow the Flag Stencilled Wall Frieze

IF YOU DECIDE TO STENCIL your child's room with Teletubbies like this, try to keep it a secret while you do it. The surprise and delight when it is revealed make all your work well worthwhile.

You have to make two-part stencils for the Teletubbies, one for their face, ears and tummy screens and one for the rest of their bodies. The only really tricky bit is when you come to stencil the head colour around the ears. You will have to hold a single ear stencil in position with the hand that is also holding the main body stencil, while you apply the paint with the other hand. It is not impossible but you need to practise, perhaps on an off-cut of lining paper beforehand.

We used emulsion paints for the blue sky and green hills, and artist's acrylic paints for all the stencils. You will need bright red, purple, a dark bluey-green, chrome yellow, white, black, brown and blue. Practise mixing colours to get lime green, grey, flesh tones and the pastel colours of the flowers. Use a lot of white paint to get enough density into pale colours such as the yellow and lime green. Only mix tiny quantities at a time or you will waste a lot of paint as so little is used for the stencilling process. Have a sheet of lining paper handy while you are stencilling, already painted with the blue and green background emulsion so that you can try out your colours as you mix.

MATERIALS

- stencil card
- craft knife
- low-tack masking tape
- emulsion (vinyl matt) paints in pale blue and bright grass green
- roller and tray or a 10cm (4in) wide paint brush
- 2.5–5cm (1–2in) wide paint brush
- fine artist's paint brush
- art and craft spray adhesive
- artist's acrylic paints in pale blue, bright grass green, bright red, purple, dark bluey-green, chrome yellow, white, black, brown and blue
- stencil brushes in a variety of sizes
- plates for mixing colours
- lining paper

Successful Stencilling

- Use as little paint as possible on your brush. Dip it in the paint and then dab off as much paint as you can on kitchen roll before applying it to the stencil.
- Apply the paint with a dabbing motion of the brush held at right angles to the wall. This is called 'pouncing'.
- Build up colour density by going over the paint again, but it is less easy to rectify excess paint that has oozed and leaked under the stencil.
- Keep plenty of rags handy to wipe your brush as you go – or wear overalls and wipe your brush on them.

Making the stencils

1 Enlarge the templates on pages 66–7 on a photocopier to the size you require: our stencilled Teletubbies ranged in size from 15cm (6in) to 25cm (10in). There are two stories running round our wall – Teletubbies marching behind Po carrying a flag, and Teletubbies running behind Laa-Laa chasing her ball. We used the same stencils in both stories except for Po who has two poses: flag-carrying and running.

2 Turn the photocopy over and draw over the back of the outline with a soft pencil. Then turn it right side up again and place it on stencil card. Rub over the outline with a coin to transfer it onto the card.

3 You will have to make a two-part stencil – one for the face, ear and tummy screen (and Po's flag) and one for the body. Cut out each stencil carefully with the craft knife. Keep the card ear that you cut out to mask off the ear when stencilling the main body. Attach it to the body stencil with a piece of masking tape to keep it safe. Tinky Winky and Po will have to keep the centres of their aerials and the squiggle in Po's flag in the same way.

Stencilling the walls

1 Mask off any skirting boards, cornices, window and door frames with masking tape. Then draw a pencil line across the wall 1m (1yd) up from the floor and paint two coats of pale blue emulsion down to just below this line. Paint two coats of bright green emulsion up to where the blue stops. With the smaller brush, paint a wavy green line for the tops of the hills and fill in with green below this line. Leave it to dry and then tidy up the line with a fine artist's brush and green paint.

2 Work out where you want to position your Teletubbies. Cut out the photocopies from which you have made your stencils and spray them with art and craft adhesive. Let them dry for a few seconds and they will be tacky enough to stick to the wall.

3 Keep the Teletubbies on or above the green hills, so that you are stencilling onto the pale blue so the background will not show through. Play around with the spacing and the angle of each Teletubby until you are happy with their positions. Leave them there until you stencil the real thing.

4 Begin with the stencil of the face, ear and screen. Align it with the photocopy on the wall, then remove the photocopy and stick the stencil in position with masking tape. Mix white, red, yellow and green acrylic paints to get flesh tones. Work most of the paint off your brush until it seems almost dry. Then hold the stencil flat against the wall with your free hand while you apply the paint through the stencil using a dabbing motion. Use the colour flat for a simple look, or experiment with shading. Continue by mixing a grey for the screen.

5 Remove the first stencil and replace it with the appropriate Teletubby body stencil. Align it with the stencilled face, and tummy screen and hold with masking tape. Mix the right colour for the body and apply the paint to the stencil as above. Laa-Laa and Dipsy will need a lot of white mixing into their colour to give enough density to cover the blue beneath.

6 When you get near the ear, hold the separate ear stencil over it to stencil around. Po and Tinky Winky have a separate stencil for the hole in their aerials as well.

7 Continue stencilling different sequences of Teletubbies around the room. Finish by stencilling bright green grass tufts and pale pastel flowers randomly across the hills.

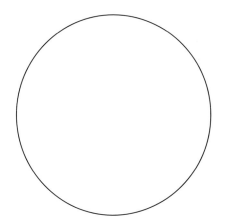

Hide-and-seek Pockets

STORAGE POCKETS THAT ARE designed for holding pairs of shoes are also useful for storing the kind of little toys that otherwise tend to disappear to the bottom of the toy box. Transformed with some felt appliqué and a collection of different fasteners, the pockets can also become a hide-and-seek game in their own right which will encourage young fingers to negotiate the intricacies of buckles and buttons, zips, laces, and snap fasteners.

This project can also be an exercise in recycling. Instead of buying new fasteners, cut the buckles and straps off an old rucksack or hold-all, and take the clasps off an outgrown pair of dungarees. Save the buttons from an old jacket, and shorten longer zips by oversewing at the desired length several times with your sewing machine stitch length set at its longest, and then cut off the remainder.

MATERIALS
- *canvas shoe storage pockets*
- *squares of felt in all the Teletubby colours plus grey, beige, brown, dark green, black, white and other bright colours*
- *pinking shears*
- *scraps of silver and orange fabrics*
- *fusible webbing*
- *felt-tipped pen in black*
- *fastenings such as: length of ribbon, large silver press stud, dungaree clip and a metal button, 10cm (4in) zip, plastic bag buckle, lace and six eyelets, covered button, plastic dog clip, flower button, 2 x D-rings, frog fastening, Velcro*
- *20cm (8in) length of 2.5cm (1in) wide elastic, dyed a bright colour*
- *20cm (8in) length, and two 10cm (4in) lengths of brightly coloured nylon strap*
- *embroidery threads in yellow and green*

Pocket 1 Cut flap (less tab) in lime green felt, using template on page 71. Fold flap in half and stitch around the open sides, 6mm (¼in) in from the raw edge. Use pinking shears to cut a decorative edge around the stitched sides of the flap. Cut length of ribbon in half and stitch the end of one half to the bottom of the flap. Stitch the flap to the canvas, 2.5cm (1in) above the top of the pocket, backstitching at the beginning and end of the row to secure. Stitch one end of the other piece of ribbon to the pocket, just below the bottom of the flap. Tie the ribbons into a bow, and snip the ends into a V.

Pocket 2 Trace Tinky Winky and a separate face, ears, eyes, tummy screen and balloon onto the paper side of fusible webbing, using the templates on page 113. Cut around them roughly and iron onto the appropriate coloured felt and silver fabric for the balloon. Cut out carefully and peel the paper backing off. Iron the figure and balloon into position on the pocket. Use the black felt-tipped pen to draw in features. Join the balloon and Tinky Winky's hand with one long stitch in yellow embroidery thread.

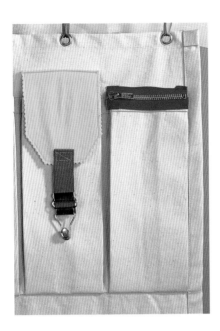

Pocket 3
Make a flap as for Pocket 1, this time in yellow felt. Dye a length of 2.5cm (1in) wide elastic red. Fold it in half and clamp dungaree clips to folded end. Fold raw edges over at other end of elastic and stitch to the bottom of the flap. Sew a shiny metal button to the pocket at the correct height to hold the buckle.

Pocket 4
Open zip and fold in raw edges at either end. Pin and then baste one side of the zip in position along top of pocket. Using a zipper foot, stitch close to the edge of zip tape backstitching at the beginning and end of the row to secure. Close the zip, then pin, baste and stitch the other side in position just above the pocket.

To the right is the second row of pockets: instructions for making them are given on this page under pockets 5 to 8.

To the left are pockets 3 and 4 which are shown on page 69 at the top right.

Pocket 5
Make a flap as for Pocket 1, this time in purple felt. Thread one end of nylon strap through one side of a snap-together buckle and stitch it down to the back of the strap. Stitch the strap to the flap along both edges. Fold the end of the strap over the top of the flap and stitch the flap to the canvas about 2.5cm (1in) above the top of the pocket. Thread another piece of strap through the other piece of the buckle. Fold the raw ends of the strap under and stitch to the pocket just below the flap.

Pocket 6
Following manufacturer's instructions, hammer two eyelets into the canvas just above the pocket. Hammer four more into the pocket. Lace with one green fluorescent lace and tie in a bow.

Pocket 7
Using fusible webbing, Laa-Laa's templates on page 115, appropriate coloured felts and the black felt-tipped pen, make and iron the figure into position on the pocket. Following the manufacturer's instructions, cover a large self-cover button with orange fabric. Make a large machine-made buttonhole near the top of the pocket with cream coloured thread. Sew the button on to the canvas behind the pocket. By buttoning and unbuttoning you can ask 'Where's Laa-Laa's ball gone?'

Pocket 8
Cut a flap as for Pocket 1 but this time in red felt with a tab. Before stitching, thread one end of the tab through the top of a plastic dog clip fastener. Fold the tab's end under the flap and stitch right around the flap. Stitch the flap to the canvas about 2.5cm (1in) above the pocket. Thread a short length of nylon strap through a D-ring, fold under the ends and stitch to the pocket, at the right level to reach the dogclip.

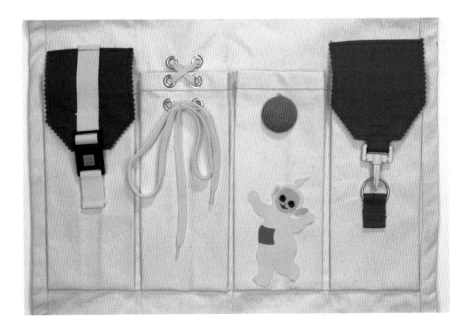

The third row of pockets: 9 to 12. Making instructions are given on this page.

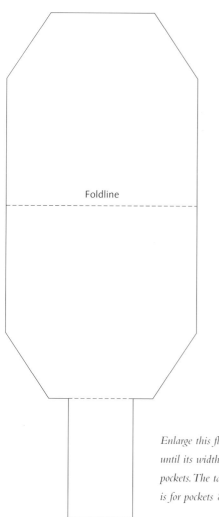

Foldline

Enlarge this flap template on a photocopier until its width matches the width of your pockets. The tab area marked at the bottom is for pockets 8 and 10 only.

Pocket 9 Draw a rectangle 10 x 20cm (4 x 8in) onto the paper side of fusible webbing. Iron onto dark green felt. Cut one end into a hill shape and iron onto pocket. Make a machine-made buttonhole at the top of the pocket. Sew a flower-shaped button onto the canvas behind the pocket. Make a flower stem and leaves from the top of the hill to the buttonhole with large stitches in green embroidery thread. Using fusible webbing, Po's templates on page 116, appropriate coloured felts and the black felt-tipped pen, make and iron the figure into position on the pocket. Using different coloured felt, make a few flower shapes and stitch onto the hillside with embroidery thread.

Pocket 10 Cut a flap as for Pocket 8 but this time in lime green felt with a tab. Before stitching, thread the tab through a D-ring, fold back under the flap and stitch the open sides. Cut a 10cm (4in) length of nylon strap and a 2.5cm (1in) length of both soft and hooked sides of Velcro. Fold both ends of the strap 1cm (1/2in) in towards the centre. Stitch the hooked side of the Velcro to one end of the strap, over the 1cm (1/2in) fold. Stitch the soft side of the Velcro to the other end of the strap. Stitch the fold to the pocket, at the right level to thread through the D-ring.

Pocket 11 Stitch the decorative loops at one end of the frog fastening to the top of the pocket by hand. Stitch the other end to the canvas above the pocket.

Pocket 12 Make a flap as for Pocket 1 but this time in yellow felt. Stitch to the canvas about 2.5cm (1in) above the pocket. Using fusible webbing, Dipsy's templates on page 114, appropriate coloured felts and the black felt-tipped pen, make and iron the figure into position on the pocket. Trace Dipsy's hat onto fusible webbing and fuse to white felt. Repeat with black felt, cutting out black cow markings. Peel off the paper backing and iron onto white hat. Sew a white Velcro spot onto the hat. Peel the paper backing off the back of the hat and iron onto pocket making sure that it will be hidden when the flap is down. Sew the hooked side of the Velcro spot onto the underside of the flap.

71

Laa-Laa's Rag Rug

RECYCLING NEVER LOOKED so beautiful as this little bedside rag rug depicting Teletubbyland with Laa-Laa and her ball. The technique for hooked rag rugs is essentially simple, and gives scope for making up wonderfully colourful pictures with different combinations of fabrics. The secret lies in building up a good collection of recycled fabrics before you start.

Knitted fabrics are the best to start with, such as T-shirts, sweatshirts, and woollen, even shrunken, jumpers, because the stretch makes them easier to handle. After you've turned out your wardrobes, and got your family and friends to do likewise, start scouring jumble and car boot sales for all the brightly coloured knitted fabrics you can find. It doesn't matter what state they're in – you're going to cut them up into thin strips anyway! You can use striped and patterned knits as well – they help to build up colour variations.

MATERIALS

- *2 pieces of hessian 10cm (4in) larger overall than the rug size*
- *chalk*
- *felt-tipped pen*
- *recycled knitted fabric such as old T-shirts, sweatshirts and knitted jumpers in blues, greens, yellows, oranges, reds, browns, creams, white and black or grey*
- *shiny fabric in grey/green*
- *rug hook or crochet hook*
- *rubber-based adhesive (optional)*

Making preparations

1 Decide on the size of your rug, and the picture you want to make. Draw a thread out of the hessian along the warp and weft to get your rug square and then draw out the dimensions of the rug and the picture on the right side of the hessian. Do this with chalk first, so that you can brush it off if you change your mind. When you are happy with it go over the chalk with the felt-tipped pen.

2 Cut strips of fabric 1–2cm (½ – ¾in) wide, depending on the thickness of the fabric. To speed up the process, fold up the garment you are cutting. If you have very sharp scissors you should then be able to cut through four or more layers at a time. Cut lots of strips of blue (or blue and white) and green; quite a bit of yellow, orange and brown, and less of the other colours.

72

Making the picture

1 Start hooking in the centre of the design and work outwards, to avoid distorting the hessian too much. To hook, hold the fabric strip behind the hessian with your spare hand. Then with your working hand, and your hook angled towards you and in the direction you are working, push down through the hessian to make a hole and catch the strip of fabric underneath. Pull one end through to the right side.

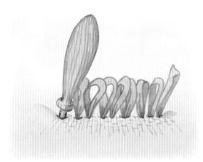 

2 Push the hook through again, but through a different hole, fairly close to the end you have pulled through. Catch the strip and pull up a little loop about 6mm (¼in) high. How densely you pack your loops depends on the thickness of the fabrics you are using but two threads of hessian apart is a good guideline. If you pack loops in too tightly the rug will hump.

3 You can control the height of the loops with your spare hand underneath. At first, work in straight lines, circles or follow the outlines of your design, and then fill in the centres.

4 Continue until you get to the end of a strip, pull it through to the right side and trim to the same height as the loops.

5 While you are working on the rug, leave it on the floor between hooking sessions so that you can stand back and see how your work is progressing.

Finishing off

1 When you have finished the whole rug, make sure all ends are pulled to the right side and trimmed. Press the rug on the right side with a hot iron protected by a tea towel.

2 Turn in the raw edges of the hessian and slipstitch to the underside of the hessian and loops. You can make it non-slip by painting the back of the rug with rubber-based adhesive. Or line it with another piece of hessian cut to the same size as the rug. Press in a hem all around and then neatly sew it to the underside of the rug by hand using strong button thread.

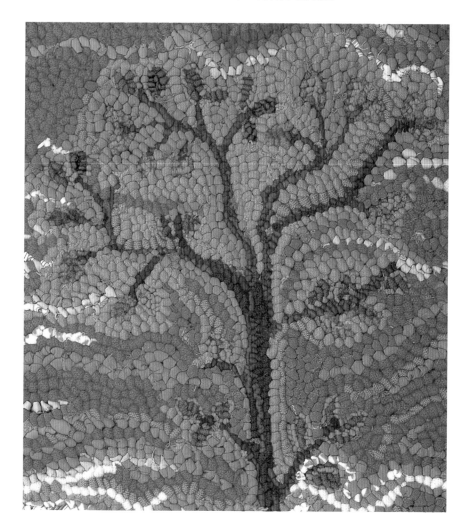

73

Teletubby Wear

Tubbied T-shirts

THERE IS A GREAT PRODUCT on the market called Image Maker made by Dylon and is available from good craft shops (see Useful Addresses). It transfers photocopied images onto plain fabric and we have used it here to customize plain white T-shirts with children's drawings of Teletubbies. One small tube of Image Maker was enough to transfer all four of the pictures here so the process is cheaper than the heat transfer process available at copy shops. It is also quite straightforward, but you have to allow time for the T-shirt to dry naturally between steps so it does take time and patience. Make sure that the artist is present when you rub away the paper and the picture begins to appear as if by magic!

MATERIALS
- *colour photocopy of picture*
- *plain white T-shirt*
- *greaseproof paper or kitchen foil*
- *tube of Dylon Image Maker*
- *paint brush*
- *kitchen roll*
- *rolling pin*

1 Choose a drawing, painting or, like the T-shirt at the top of the pile below, a picture made on a child's computer graphics programme. Take it to a copy shop and make a colour photocopy enlarged or reduced in size as required. If there are any words on the drawing, have the photocopy reversed or they will come out back to front on the T-shirt.

2 Areas of white show as a shiny plastic coating on the fabric so where the artist has left a lot of white space, cut around the individual figures as close to the drawing as possible. If the whole page is filled with colour, trim off the white edges of the photocopy.

3 Insert a layer of greaseproof paper or kitchen foil between the front and back of the T-shirt to stop the image bleeding through onto the back. Also find a place where the T-shirt can lie to dry undisturbed for several hours and spread out a layer of newspaper to protect your surface. Arrange the T-shirt on your work surface.

4 Lay the chosen photocopy face up on another sheet of greaseproof paper or kitchen foil. Squeeze a generous amount of Image Maker onto the photocopy and spread it evenly over the whole image with a paint brush. Use it quite thickly, and make sure that it is spread right up to and over the edges of the copy. Then place it face down in position on the T-shirt. Place some kitchen roll over the top and smooth it down with a rolling pin until you are sure that all areas are in contact with the fabric. Leave it to dry thoroughly, preferably overnight.

5 When it is completely dry, immerse the whole T-shirt in cold water. Wait a while for the paper to become thoroughly saturated and then, using a sponge or flannel, begin to gently rub off the paper. As the paper comes away, so the image will slowly appear, transferred perfectly in every detail onto the T-shirt. Hang it up to dry naturally.

6 Seal the transfer with another thin coat of Image Maker. This leaves a shiny plastic coating on the image, so try only to paint it over the transfer.

Tubby Aerial Hats

THESE HATS ARE SURPRISINGLY quick to make and the aerials are re-inforced with bendy hair rollers so they really do stand up! (These rollers usually come in packets of five and are available in chemists and supermarkets.) The hats are made of felt which is an extremely versatile material and easily available from craft shops in exactly the right Teletubby colours. It's a very easy fabric to handle as it doesn't fray and it can be sponged clean. Buy the felt by the metre (yard) rather than in squares because the rolled brim needs a long length. If you can't get hold of the right colours from a roll, join together three squares of felt to get the length required for the brim.

You will notice that one of the design features of these hats is that the seams are all finished on the outside. This is no accident – it makes the hat far more comfortable to wear; always of prime importance when you are four years old.

MATERIALS
- *1cm (½in) squared paper*
- *20cm (8in) (or 8 squares) of felt in red, purple, yellow or lime green*
- *tailor's chalk*
- *pinking shears*
- *rubber-based adhesive*
- *1 bendy hair roller*

Making the hat

1 Scale up the pattern pieces on page 84 onto squared paper (see page 112). Three sizes are given, so choose the most appropriate. Cut out the pieces and use as templates to draw around with tailor's chalk onto the felt. Cut out 6 crowns, 1 aerial, 1 rolled brim and two 4.5cm (1¾in) diameter reinforcing circles.

2 Leaving a 5mm (¼in) seam allowance and with edges aligned, stitch all 6 crown pieces together along the curved sides, backstitching to start and finish. Don't worry too much about the points at the top meeting perfectly as they will be covered by the aerial. Trim each seam close to the stitchline with pinking shears.

3 Align the two short ends of the brim piece and stitch with a 5mm (¼in) seam allowance to form a ring. Fold the brim in half so the two long sides meet and with the wrong side inside.

4 Turn the crown inside out (pinked seams on the inside) and pin the folded brim around the outside of the bottom edge of the crown so all three raw edges are aligned. Leaving a 1cm (½in) seam allowance, stitch the brim and crown together. Trim the seam close to the stitchline with pinking shears and turn the hat right side out. Turn up the brim.

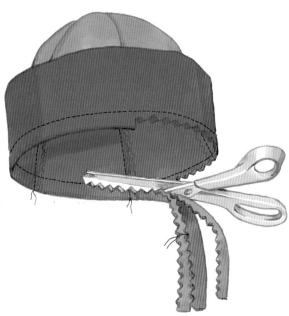

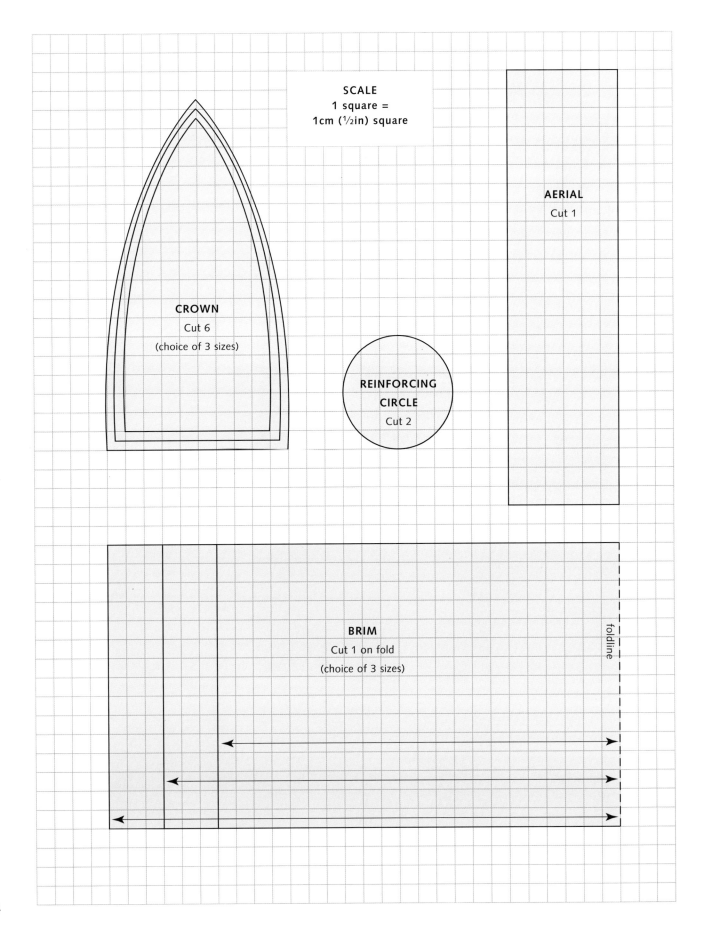

SCALE
1 square =
1cm (½in) square

AERIAL
Cut 1

CROWN
Cut 6
(choice of 3 sizes)

REINFORCING
CIRCLE
Cut 2

BRIM
Cut 1 on fold
(choice of 3 sizes)

foldline

Making the aerial

1. Brush some rubber-based adhesive along two long sides of the aerial piece. Then lay the bendy roller on one glued edge, with 1.5cm (⅝in) of felt at either end. Roll the felt around the roller and press down the other glued side to hold. Slip stitch neatly down the glued join.

2. Finish the end of the aerial by making a row of tiny running stitches around the end of the felt, pulling it tight so that the felt gathers up. Wind the thread around the end and finish it off securely. Trim the end as near to the stitches as you dare. Cut into the felt at the other end of the aerial dividing it into six segments.

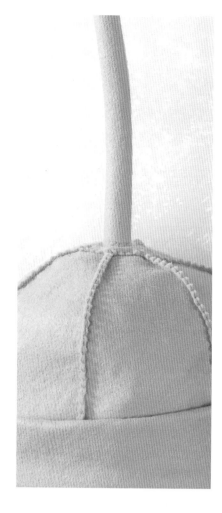

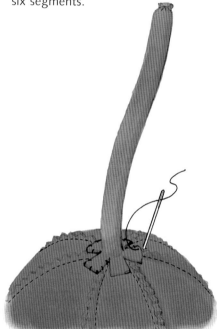

3. Stitch each segment down to the top of the hat. Your stitches don't have to be neat as they will be hidden under the reinforcing circle, but you do have to go up and down both sides of each little segment so that the aerial is held as upright as possible on top of the hat.

4. Cut a 1cm (½in) diameter hole in the centre of one of the reinforcing rings. Thread the aerial through this hole. Don't worry if it seems too small, it is supposed to be a tight fit and the felt will stretch. Then pull the circle to the base of the aerial and stitch it down by hand around the inner and outer edges.

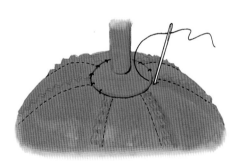

5. Turn the hat inside out and stitch the other reinforcing circle in place underneath the aerial with a spiral of running stitches.

6. Depending on what colour your hat is, bend the aerial into its appropriate shape, and, in the case of Tinky Winky's and Po's, stitch the end in place securely.

Dipsy's Hat

DIPSY'S HAT IS A TREMENDOUS fashion statement and you'll be amazed at how the true Teletubby fan will, completely unprompted, know exactly what it is when presented with one. Any child will long to include this stylish topper in their dressing-up wardrobe. The real Dipsy's hat has a hole in the top to fit his aerial through but since we don't know any real children with aerials and it makes its construction slightly more complicated, we've omitted this design detail. The hat is made of fun fur and has a brightly coloured cotton drill lining.

MATERIALS
- *1cm (1/2in) squared paper*
- *felt-tipped pen or tailor's chalk*
- *50cm (20in) black and white cow fun fur*
- *25cm (10in) cotton drill in bright orange*
- *75cm (30in) medium-weight iron-on interfacing*

Making the outside of the hat

1 Scale up the pattern pieces on pages 88–9 onto squared paper (see page 112). Cut out the pieces and use as templates to draw around with a felt-tipped pen or tailor's chalk onto the wrong side of the fabric. Out of fun fur, cut 2 circles for the brim (without cutting out the inner circle) and 1 crown and 1 top. Repeat with the interfacing. Out of the cotton drill lining fabric, cut 1 crown and 1 top.

2 Iron the interfacing onto the wrong side of all the fun fur pieces.

3 With right sides together, pin and baste the two brim circles together. Remove the pins and machine stitch all around the outer edge, leaving a 1cm (1/2in) seam allowance. Don't trim or snip this seam allowance because that will detract from the slightly wavy nature of Dipsy's brim. Now cut through both layers of fabric to remove the inner circle of the brim. Remove the basting stitches and turn the brim right side out.

4 With right sides together, pin and baste together the two short ends of the crown piece to form a ring. Remove the pins and stitch, leaving a 1cm (1/2in) seam allowance and backstitching at the beginning and end of the seam. Remove the basting stitches and press the seam open.

5 With right sides together, pin and baste the top piece to the wider edge of the crown. Remove the pins and stitch, leaving a 1cm (1/2in) seam allowance. Remove the basting stitches, press this seam open, and then turn the crown right side out.

6 Put the crown top down on a table and with right sides facing, pin and baste both layers of the brim around the open end of the crown. Stitch together firmly, leaving a 1cm (1/2in) seam allowance. Remove the basting stitches and press this seam to the inside of the hat.

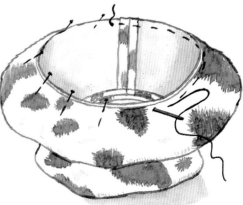

Finishing the hat

1 Repeat steps 4 and 5 using the crown and top pieces cut out of cotton drill for the lining of the hat. Press a 1cm (½in) seam allowance towards the wrong side of the fabric around the open end of the crown. Turn the lining inside out.

2 Insert the lining into the crown of the hat so the wrong sides are together. Slipstitch to attach the lining to the hat around the base of the crown so that all seam allowances are enclosed.

3 Machine stitch around the base of the crown through the lining and fur to reinforce your hand sewing. Finally, machine around the brim about 1cm (½in) in from the outer edge to hold the two layers of brim together.

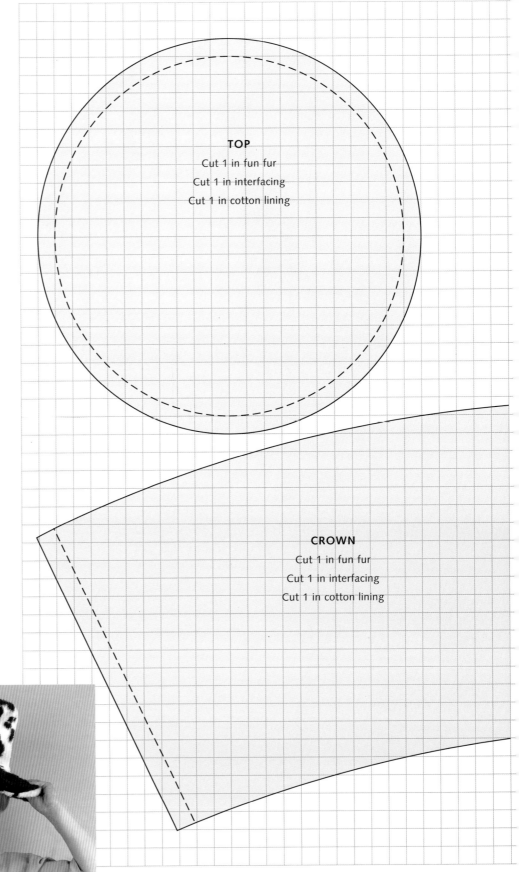

TOP
Cut 1 in fun fur
Cut 1 in interfacing
Cut 1 in cotton lining

CROWN
Cut 1 in fun fur
Cut 1 in interfacing
Cut 1 in cotton lining

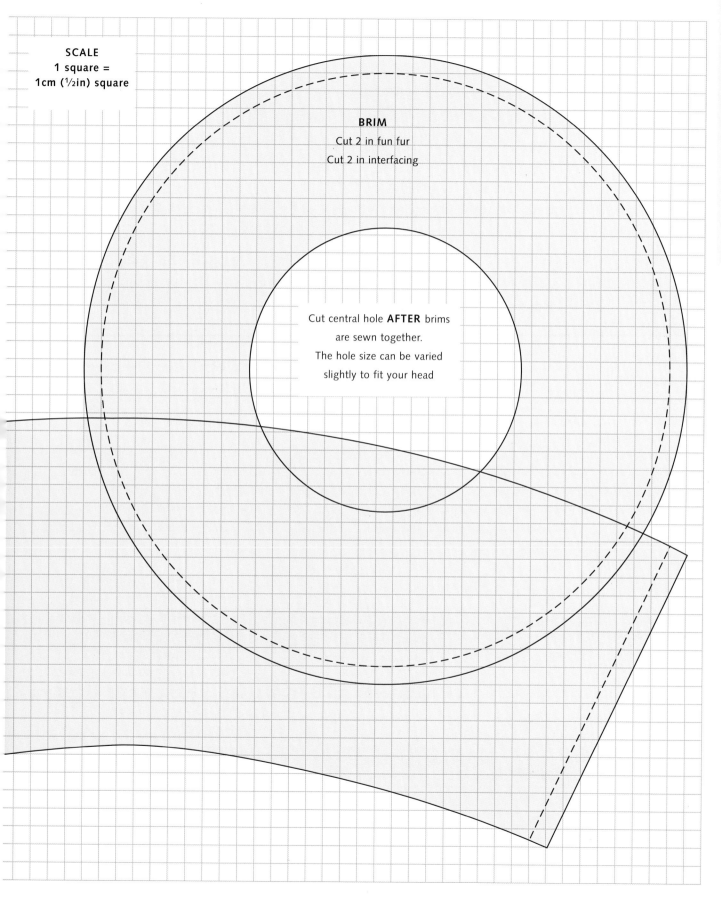

SCALE
1 square =
1cm (½in) square

BRIM
Cut 2 in fun fur
Cut 2 in interfacing

Cut central hole **AFTER** brims
are sewn together.
The hole size can be varied
slightly to fit your head

Po's Back Pack

THIS LITTLE BACKPACK is made out of red ripstop nylon with Po's face drawn onto the flap with a waterproof marker and an aerial that doubles as a carrying handle. Ripstop nylon is the material that kites are made of and is available by mail order from kite suppliers (see Useful Addresses). It feels like paper but is incredibly strong, impossible to tear and easy to sew.

Unfortunately, it is only available in 50cm (½yd) lengths which means that you will have a lot of grey and white left over after you've cut out the pocket and face pieces. But it is relatively cheap so if you can't club together with friends to share with, perhaps you could grade the pattern up and make a smart grey and white backback for yourself!

MATERIALS
- *50cm (½yd) ripstop nylon in red*
- *4 metal eyelets*
- *tailor's chalk*
- *scraps of ripstop nylon in grey and white*
- *sticky tape*
- *permanent markers in brown and black*
- *Velcro spot or 2.5cm (1in) strip of Velcro*
- *10cm (4in) square piece of lightweight (2oz) polyester wadding*
- *2m (2yd) cord*

Cutting out

Out of red ripstop

1 body measuring 27 x 68cm (10½ x 26¾in)

2 straps measuring 42 x 8cm (16½ x 3in)

2 aerial pieces measuring 10cm (4in) square

2 head pieces taken from the template overleaf

Out of grey ripstop

1 pocket measuring 13 x 15cm (5 x 6in)

Out of white ripstop

1 circle for the face following the template overleaf

2 ear pieces taken from the template overleaf

Making the bag

1. On the red body piece mark a spot 5.5cm (2¼in) from each corner. On the floor hammer in the eyelets, following the manufacturer's instructions.

2. Draw in the outline of the pocket position on the bag piece with tailor's chalk, centring it 21cm (8¼in) down from one short end. Turn in a 1cm (½in) double hem along one long side of the grey pocket piece and machine. Then stitch the pocket in place on the bag with a double row of top stitching, turning in a 1cm (½in) seam allowance all round the other three sides as you go. You can't really use pins on ripstop as they will leave tiny holes, so if you find it impossible to stitch on the pocket without, use sticky tape to hold it in position. Start stitching and, as you get close to the tape, remove it.

3. Take the two strap pieces and fold them in half so the two long sides are aligned. Leaving a 1cm (½in) seam allowance, stitch down the length of each strap. Turn the straps right side out and top stitch down each side about 5mm (¼in) in.

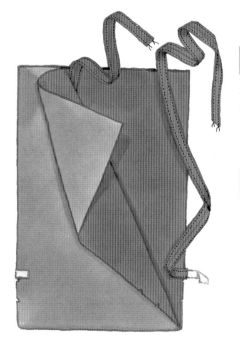

4 Fold the bag piece in half with right sides together and cut notches on each side seam 4cm (1½in) and 7cm (2¾in) up from the fold. On each side, align one raw end of each strap with the sides between the two layers and above the 7cm (2¾in) notch. Use a piece of sticky tape to hold each strap in position.

5 Leaving a 1cm (½in) seam allowance, stitch up each side seam of the bag, machining over the ends of each strap and backstitching securely at the open end of the bag.

6 At the folded end of the bag, fold each corner into a point and stitch across at right angles to the side seam at the level of the notch you made 4cm (1½in) up from the fold. Back stitch at either end of this seam, and, leaving a 1cm (½in) seam allowance, trim the corner off the bag.

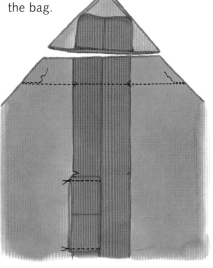

7 Fold a 1cm (½in) allowance around the open end and stitch close to the raw edge to hold it. Then fold a 3.5cm (1⅓in) hem and stitch close to the hemmed edge. Turn the bag right side out.

Making the face

1 Lay the white face piece over the template opposite and trace the facial features using the brown and black permanent markers.

2 Stitch the soft side of the Velcro spot or strip onto the bottom edge of one red head piece, remembering to leave a 5mm (¼in) seam allowance. With right sides together, stitch together the two red head pieces, leaving the square part at the top open. Trim the seam allowance as close as possible to the stitching and turn the head right side out.

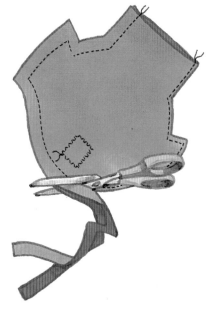

3 Stitch the white face piece into position on the side without the Velcro, using a tiny zigzag stitch to oversew the raw edge of the white face. Do the same with the ears. Use sticky tape to hold the white ripstop in place but pull it away just before you stitch over it.

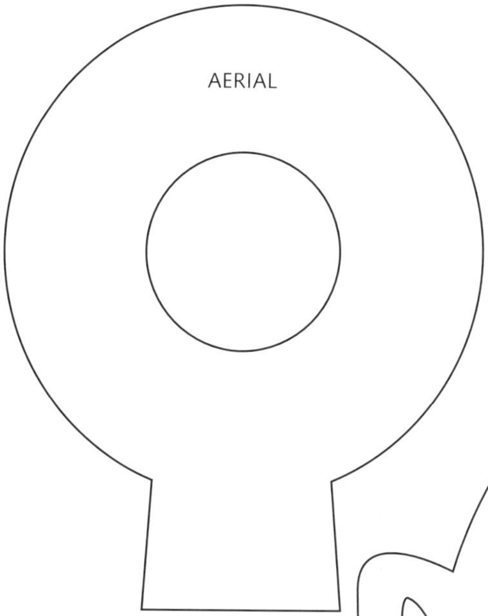

AERIAL

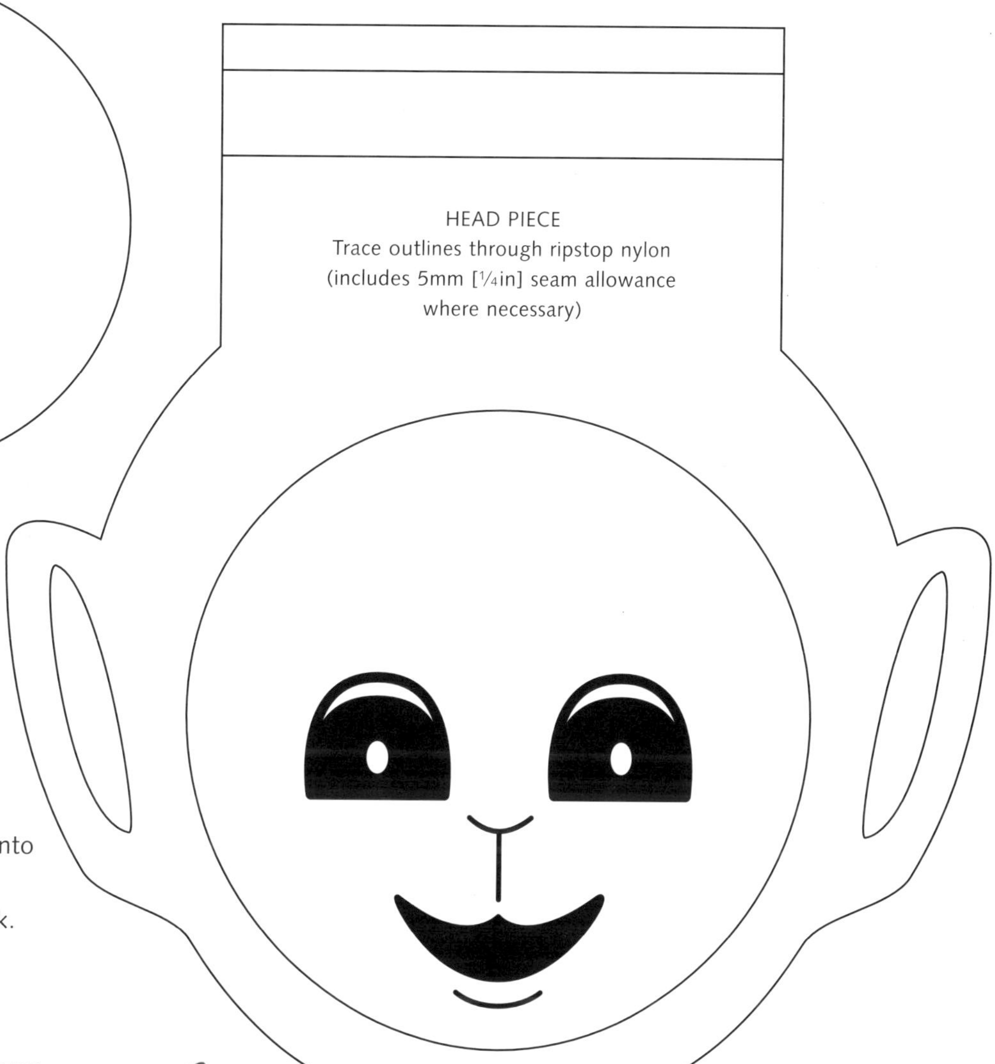

HEAD PIECE
Trace outlines through ripstop nylon
(includes 5mm [¼in] seam allowance
where necessary)

Making the aerial

1 Trace the aerial (above) onto one of the 10cm (4in) squares of red ripstop with chalk. Sandwich the piece of polyester wadding between that piece of ripstop and the other. Machine through all layers with a tiny zigzag stitch following your chalked outline. Cut around the aerial close to the stitchline. The wadding gives the aerial just enough body to help it to stand up.

2 On the back of the bag, find the centre point by folding it in half and mark it with chalk. Lay the two loose ends of the straps, the aerial and the flap of the bag over that centre point and the bag's hem and stitch across it parallel to the stitching on the hem. Fold the flap upwards and machine again, 1cm (½in) up from the previous stitching, neatly backstitching at the beginning and end of the row to secure firmly.

3 Cut the cord in two. Then, using a safety pin pinned through one end, thread the cord through an eyelet and all the way round to the other eyelet on that side. Repeat with the other cord on the other side. To finish, knot the ends of each cord together and trim the ends to neaten.

93

Tubbytronic Rain Capes

RAINY DAYS WILL be much more fun from now on when you make one of these showerproof capes out of ripstop nylon. The grey tummy screen has side openings to form a useful pocket and when the hood is tied up snugly under the chin, the aerial, which is given a little body by a layer of polyester wadding, will stand up on top. Don't be put off by the ripstop nylon – it really is terribly easy to handle.

MATERIALS

- 2cm (³⁄₄in) squared paper
- tailor's chalk
- 1.25m (1¼yd) ripstop nylon in the appropriate colour
- 30cm (12in) ripstop nylon in grey
- 10cm (4in) polyester wadding
- sticky tape
- 2 metal eyelets
- 1m (1yd) cord

Making the cape

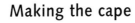

1 Scale up the pattern pieces on pages 96–7 onto squared paper (see page 112). Cut out the pieces and use them as templates to draw around with tailor's chalk. Out of ripstop nylon in the appropriate colour cut 1 rain cape piece, 2 hood pieces, 1 drawstring strip and 2 aerial pieces. Cut 1 grey ripstop nylon pocket. Cut 1 aerial square out of polyester wadding.

2 Leaving a 1cm (½in) seam allowance, sew together the centre fronts of the cape from notch A to the hem. Turn the cape right side out and, folding both seam allowances in the same direction, top stitch them down 8mm (⅓in) from the seamline. Fold in a 5mm (¼in) double hem around the bottom edge, machining it down as you fold.

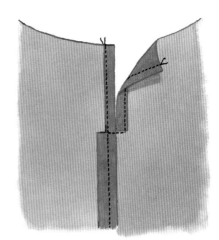

3 Above notch A, fold under a 5mm (¼in) double hem on both sides of the opening and top stitch close to the fold starting at the neckline on one side, down to the beginning of the centre seam. Leaving the needle in the work, lift the foot and turn the work so that you can continue stitching up the other side of the opening, back to the neckline.

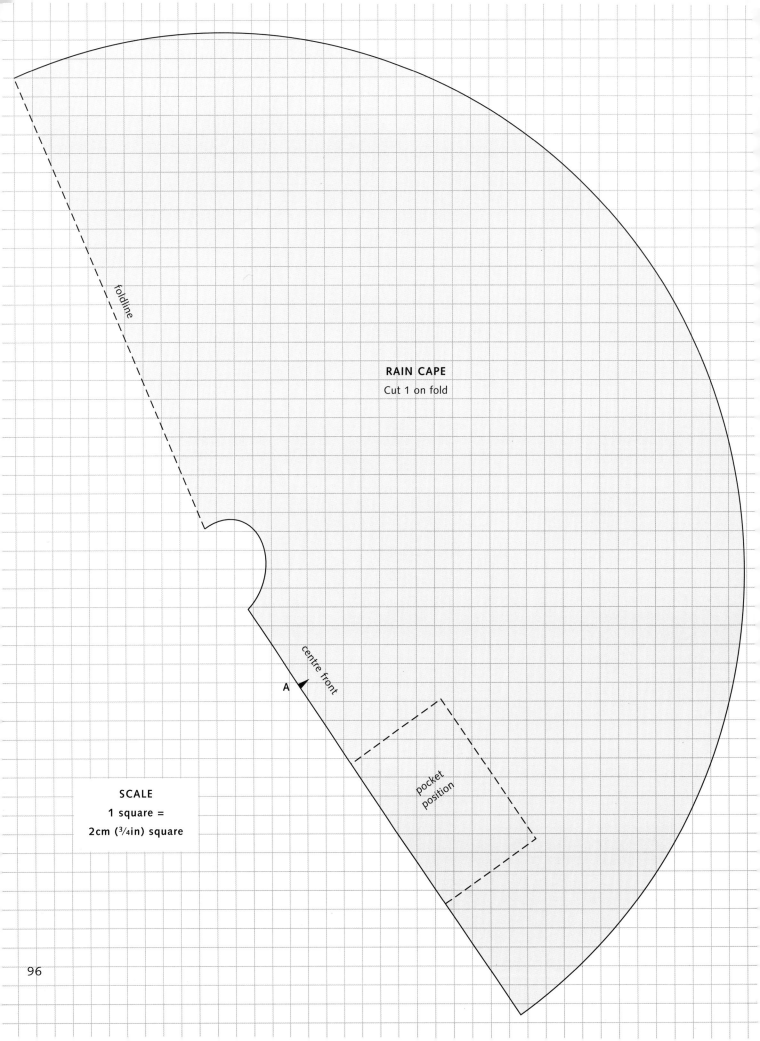

RAIN CAPE
Cut 1 on fold

foldline

centre front

A

pocket
position

SCALE
1 square =
2cm (¾in) square

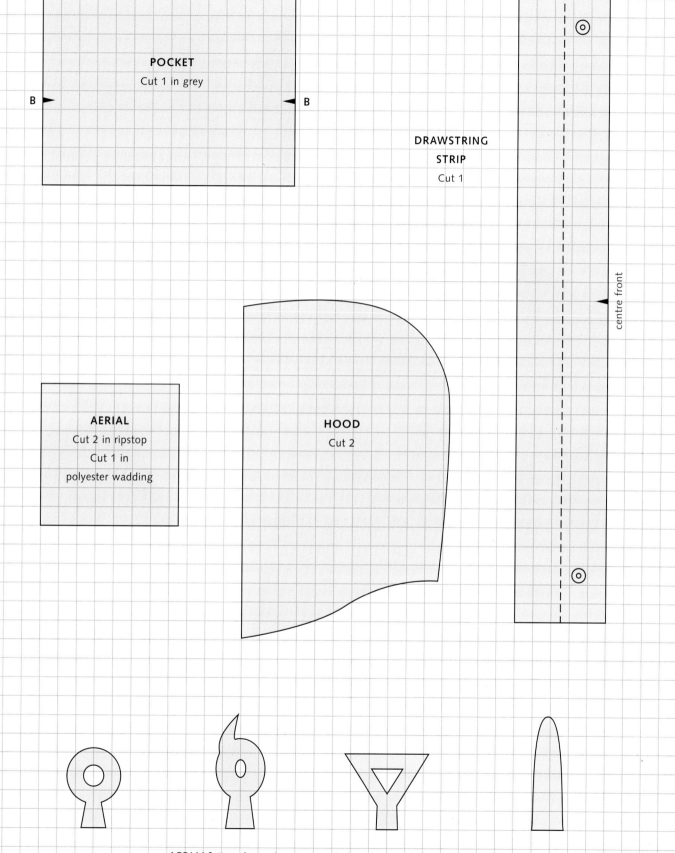

POCKET
Cut 1 in grey

B ◄   ► B

**DRAWSTRING
STRIP
Cut 1**

centre front

AERIAL
Cut 2 in ripstop
Cut 1 in
polyester wadding

HOOD
Cut 2

AERIALS Transfer outline to one of the ripstop aerial squares

Making the pocket

1. On the grey pocket piece, turn in a 1cm (½in) hem on each short side above notch B. Make a double row of top-stitching.

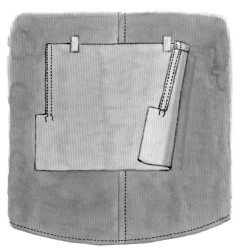

2. Fold a 1cm (½in) hem along the top of the pocket and position on the centre front of the cape, over the centre seam. Don't use pins as they will leave holes in the ripstop – instead you can use little pieces of sticky tape to hold the pocket in position. Stitch in place with a double row of top stitching along the top of the pocket, removing the tape just before you stitch over it.

3. Fold in a 1cm (½in) hem along the bottom half of the side seams and the bottom edge. Stitch from notch B, down the side, along the bottom and up the other side to the second notch B and back again to make a double row of top stitching.

Making the hood and aerial

1 On the cape piece, stay stitch 1cm (½in) in from the neckline. Snip into the seam allowance all the way around the neckline.

2 For the aerial transfer an outline of the appropriate aerial from page 97 onto one of the aerial squares with chalk. Sandwich the polyester wadding between the two aerial pieces of ripstop and pin at the sides. Then, following the chalk outline, stitch the aerial shape through all three layers. Trim away the layers close to the stitchline.

3 Stitch the curved edges of the two hood pieces together taking a 1cm (½in) seam allowance. Fold the seam allowances to one side, turn the work right side up and top stitch 8mm (⅓in) in from the seamline. Place the aerial on the right side of the hood, at the top of the curved seam. Stay stitch to hold it in place.

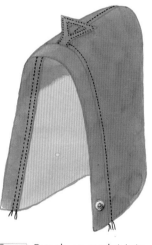

4 Punch an eyelet into either end of the drawstring strip following the manufacturer's instructions. Fold the strip in half lengthways and, leaving a 1cm (½in) seam allowance, stitch the strip to the hood. Fold the seam allowances in towards the hood and top stitch 8mm (⅓in) in from the seamline to hold, making sure you leave the aerial free.

5 To help the aerial stand up, fold it towards the back of the hood and stitch over the base, close to the seam line.

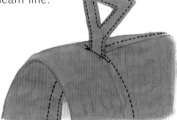

6 Stitch the hood to the cape, spreading out the snips to straighten the curve of the neckline. Fold the seam allowances towards the hood and top stitch 8mm (⅓in) from the seamline. Thread the cord through the eyelets so the hood can be tied under the chin.

Tinky Winky's Bag and Tubby Toast Purse

EVERYONE KNOWS THAT Tinky Winky likes to keep a piece of tubby toast inside his bag in case he gets a bit peckish. But not everyone will know instantly that this piece of tubby toast in our cotton bag has been cunningly disguised as a purse and is sewn into the bag for safekeeping with a length of satin ribbon.

The closure for the bag looks like a button but so that it is easy for small fingers to open and close, the button is in fact a large metal press stud. It is very simply attached with a hammer!

MATERIALS
- *1cm (½in) squared paper*
- *soft pencil or tailor's chalk*
- *30cm (12in) cotton fabric in bright red*
- *10cm (4in) cotton fabric in gold*
- *iron-on interfacing*
- *1 large metal press stud*
- *2 squares of felt in dark brown*
- *1 x 10cm (4in) zip*
- *1 square of felt in beige*
- *20cm (8in) satin ribbon*

Making the bag

1 Scale up the pattern pieces overleaf onto squared paper (see page 112). Cut out the pieces and use as templates to draw around with a soft pencil or tailor's chalk. Out of red cotton, cut 2 bag pieces and 2 strips for handles; out of gold cotton, cut 4 clasp pieces. Out of iron-on interfacing, cut 2 clasp pieces without seam allowances.

2 With right sides together, fold one bag piece in half with the two short sides aligned. Leaving a 1cm (½in) seam allowance, stitch down both side seams starting at notches A and ending at the bottom corners. Press the seams open, also pressing the seam allowances above the notches. Repeat Step 2 for the other bag piece.

3 Open out one corner at the bottom of the bag so that the side seam is aligned with the bottom fold (see Step 6 on page 92). Stitch across the corner, about 3cm (1¼in) up from the bottom of the side seam, back stitching at the beginning and end to secure your stitches. Cut off the corner, leaving a 1cm (½in) seam allowance below the seam you have just made. Repeat for the other corners on both bag pieces.

4 Turn one bag the wrong side out and insert into the other one. Pin the folded edges together above the notches. Starting at one top edge, stitch close to the edge down to the notch, leave the needle in the work and lift the presser foot. Swivel the work right round and stitch up the other side to the top of the bag again. Repeat on the other side of the bag.

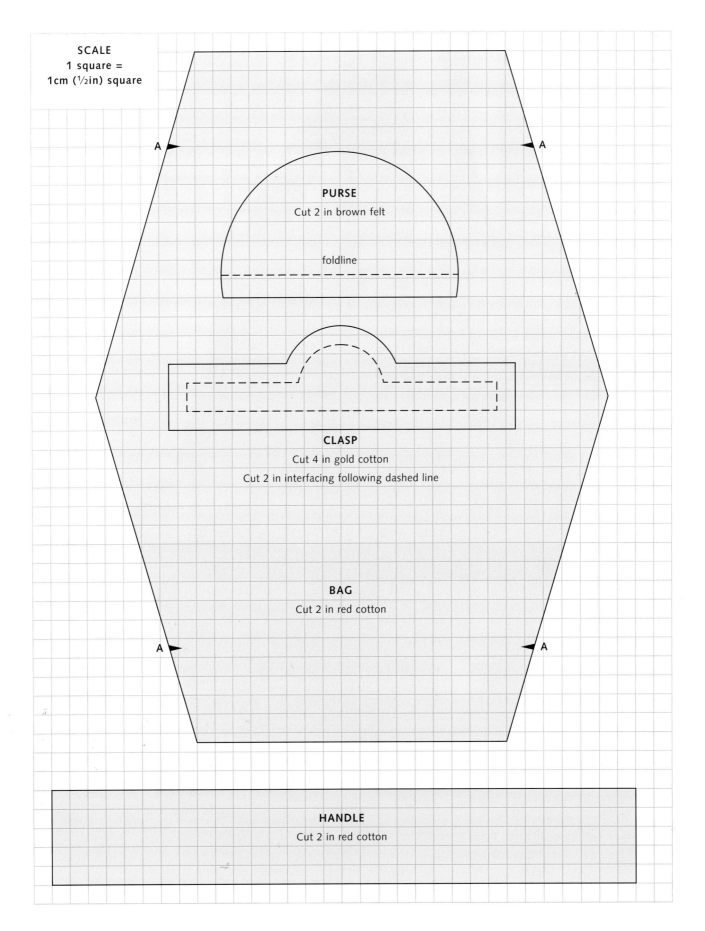

SCALE
1 square =
1cm (½in) square

A ►

◄ A

PURSE
Cut 2 in brown felt

foldline

CLASP
Cut 4 in gold cotton
Cut 2 in interfacing following dashed line

BAG
Cut 2 in red cotton

A ►

◄ A

HANDLE
Cut 2 in red cotton

Adding the details

1 Take one handle strip and fold in 1cm (½in) down each long side. Then fold it in half lengthways, wrong sides facing. Put the folded edges together and top stitch close to the edge. Repeat for the other handle.

2 Iron the interfacing pieces onto two of the clasp pieces. With right sides together, lay one interfaced piece on top of a piece without interfacing and pin together. Insert each end of a handle strip into either side of the clasp 2cm (¾in) in from the outside corners and pin.

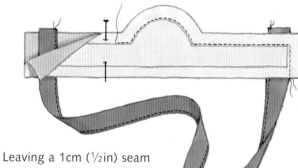

3 Leaving a 1cm (½in) seam allowance, stitch around the top edge of the clasp, making sure you sew right over the ends of the handle. Trim the seam allowance, particularly closely across the corners and around the hump in the middle. Turn the clasp piece right side out and press. Press in a 1cm (½in) seam allowance along the bottom raw edges. Repeat for the other clasp piece.

4 Pin each clasp piece to the top of the bag, enclosing all raw edges. Pin and baste. Top stitch close to the edge all round the clasp piece, making sure that the stitches catch in the clasp edge on the inside of the bag too.

5 Following the manufacturer's instructions, hammer a large metal press stud into position on the clasp.

Making the purse

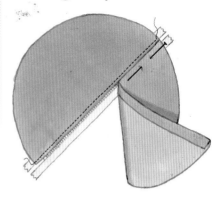

1 Cut 2 semi-circles in dark brown felt following the template given opposite. Press in a 1cm (½in) seam allowance along both straight edges. Butt the folded edge of one semi-circle close to the teeth of the zip and machine stitch. Repeat for the other semi-circle on the other side of the zip.

2 Cut two more circles in brown felt to match the zipped back from step 1. Trim one so that it is marginally smaller and draw a face of tubbytoast onto it with tailor's chalk. Cut out the eyes and mouth. Then cut an 8cm (3¼in) square of beige felt and lay it underneath the face and stitch through both layers all around the eyes and mouth very close to the edge.

3 Put the remaining felt circle under the face and stitch the two circles together close to the edge of the smaller circle.

4 With wrong sides together, put the back and front of the purse together and stitch all around the outer edge, just outside the inner circle. Trim close to the stitching all the way round. Stitch a length of satin ribbon into the inside of the bag and tie the other end to the zip slider.

Custard Splats on my Toes

BRIGHT PINK CUSTARD-SPLATTERED gym shoes should be on the wish list of most Teletubby fans and as they are so easy to make, those wishes can become reality overnight. Children will love watching the final hairdrying process when the pink paint starts to puff up in front of their eyes.

MATERIALS
- *pair of black, elasticated gym shoes*
- *puff fabric paint in fluorescent pink*
- *hairdryer*

1 Puff fabric paint comes in a little plastic bottle with a nozzle so that you can apply the paint directly without a paint brush. Draw the amoeba-like outline shape of a few custard splats onto the shoe upper. It is quite runny so keep the splats on the flattest part of the shoe to avoid runs. Leave the shoes to dry, preferably overnight.

2 With a hairdryer at its hottest setting, blow hot air onto each custard splat. Hold the dryer very close to the shoe until the paint reaches an optimum temperature. This can take several minutes, but eventually the edges of the splat will start to change to a lighter colour and slowly rise up. Keep going until all the paint has puffed up.

Teletubby Tutu

HERE IS ANOTHER very quick and easy project for the dressing-up box. The tutu is made to wrap over and do up with a long strip of Velcro at either end of the waistband which means it will continue to fit a growing child for several years.

MATERIALS
- *2m (2yd) net in pale pink*
- *70cm (28in) of 7cm (2¾in) wide satin ribbon in pink*
- *matching sewing thread*
- *10cm (4in) Velcro*

1 Cut along the net, dividing it into three 2m (2yd) long strips. Stitch all the layers together along one long side. Trim the layers of net on the skirt to the length you require – ours are 30cm, 33cm and 36cm (12in, 13in and 14in).

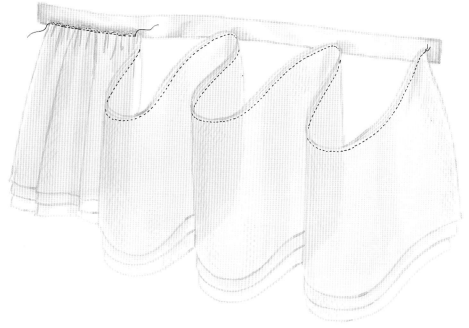

2 Leaving a 1cm (½in) allowance at each end, fold the ribbon in half and then in quarters. On the wrong side, mark with a pencil where each fold lies. Then fold the net in half and then in quarters and press the top of the folds with the iron. Open the folds out and pin the net to the wrong side of the ribbon, aligning the pressed marks on the net to the pencil marks on the ribbon.

3 Starting 1cm (½in) in from the end of the ribbon, stitch the net to the ribbon, pleating the net as you go to gather up the excess.

4 With the wrong side facing up, press in 1cm (½in) at either end of the ribbon then press the whole ribbon in half lengthways. Sandwich the net inside the folded ribbon and stitch down one short end of the folded ribbon and all along the length and up the other short end.

5 Sew the soft side of the Velcro to the wrong side of the waistband at one end, and the hooked side to the right side at the right point to fit the child's waist.

The perfect fashion statement: a brightly coloured tutu that you can wear with almost anything.

Tubby Custard Protectors

A TUBBY CUSTARD PROTECTOR is just the job for messy activities like painting, gardening or baking. It's made out of PVC fabric which is widely available, mainly for making wipedown tablecloths. The silver stretch PVC fabric that is used for the binding is quite expensive but since it adds the essential tubbytronic touch to the apron and you don't need very much, it's worth the extra expense. To make the stretch PVC easier to sew on a sewing machine look out for a Teflon-coated presser foot that is designed to slide over plastics and leather. If you haven't got a Teflon foot, or can't find silver stretch PVC, you could use silver lamé or silver grey satin instead.

MATERIALS
- 2cm (³⁄₄in) squared paper
- tailor's chalk
- 50cm (¹⁄₂yd) PVC tablecloth fabric
- 30cm (12in) stretch PVC fabric in silver
- 30cm (12in) polyester wadding
- rubber-based adhesive
- sticky tape
- sewing thread
- Teflon presser foot on your sewing machine
- 2 press studs

Making the apron

1 Scale up the pattern pieces overleaf onto squared paper (see page 112). Cut out the pieces and use as templates to draw around with tailor's chalk. Cut out the apron and four tabs in PVC. Cut sufficient strips of silver fabric 7cm (2³⁄₄in) wide so when joined they fit around the outside of the apron and the inside of the neck.

2 Cut some strips of wadding 4cm (1¹⁄₂in) wide and glue them down the centre of the wrong side of the silver strips using little dabs of rubber adhesive.

3 Leaving a 1.5cm (⁵⁄₈in) seam allowance and with the right side of the binding against the wrong side of the apron, stitch the binding to the apron. Start at the back of the apron, leaving 3cm (1¹⁄₄in) of binding free at the beginning and stop when you get back to within 5cm (2in) of where you started stitching.

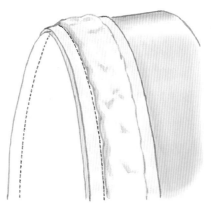

4 Fold in a 1.5cm (⁵⁄₈in) seam allowance along the other side of the silver strip and then fold the whole strip in half lengthways over the edge of the apron. You can't pin through the PVC or you will make holes, so, if necessary, hold the binding in place with pieces of sticky tape which you rip off just before stitching over them.

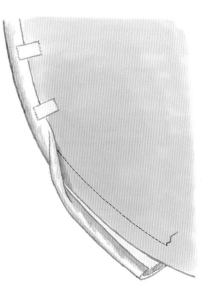

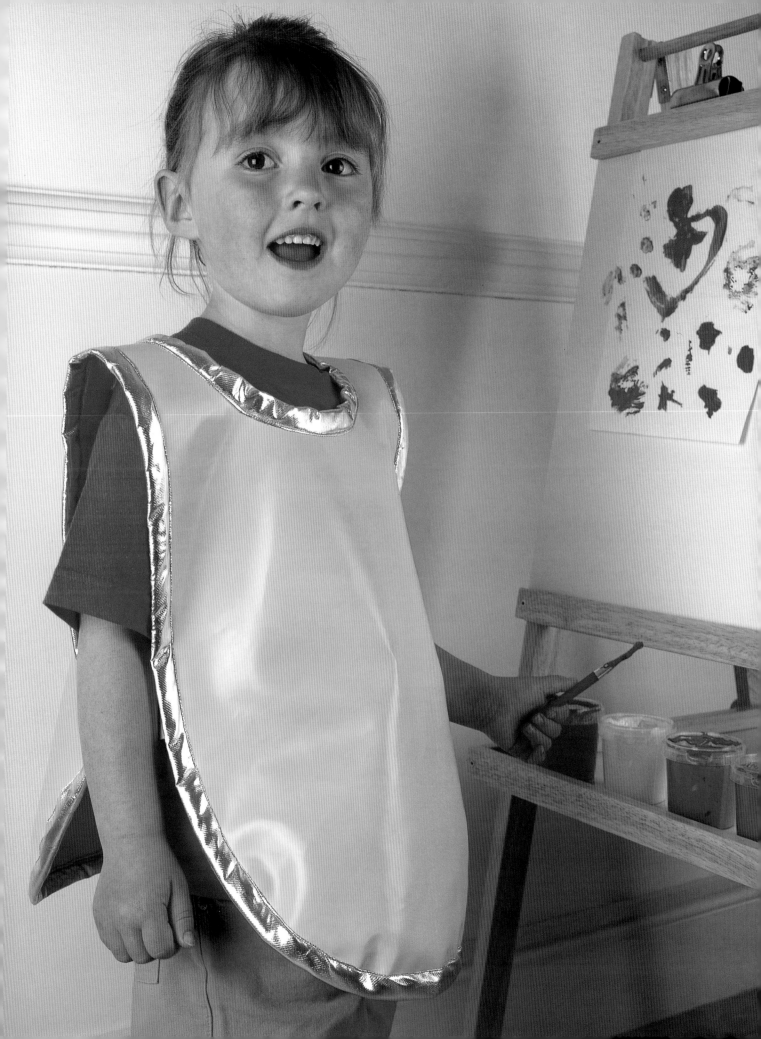

5 Still leaving the ends of the binding free, turn the work right side up and start to topstitch the binding down. This is where you will really need your Teflon presser foot and, if the silver fabric is still sticking, it may need extra encouragement with a sprinkling of talcum powder.

Attaching the tabs

1 Mark the position for the press stud on each of the four PVC tabs with a felt-tipped pen. Using the manufacturer's instructions, punch and hammer in the press studs.

2 Use small pieces of sticky tape to hold the tabs in position on either side of the apron. Check that the back and front tabs meet when the apron is folded in half at the shoulders. Stitch in place just behind the binding, ripping off the sticky tape as you get to it and back stitching at the beginning and end of the row to secure.

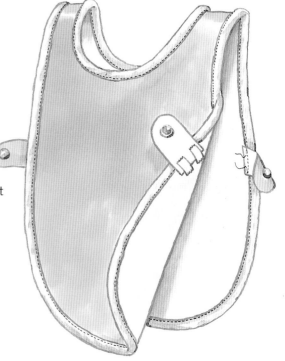

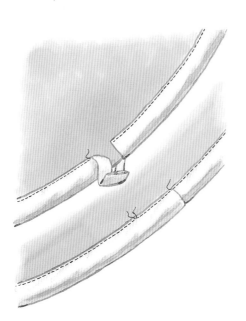

6 To finish the ends of the binding, trim the end 3cm (1¼in) beyond the start. Cut away the wadding. Fold in 1cm (½in) at the end of the binding, slide the start of the binding under the folded end and stitch over the join.

7 Follow steps 3 to 6, starting on page 108 for binding the neckline.

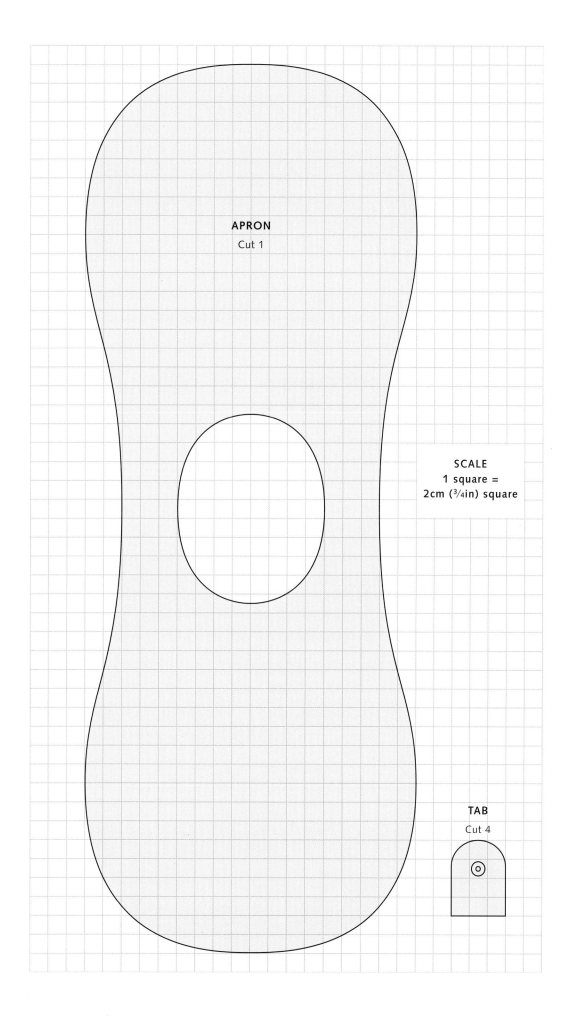

APRON
Cut 1

SCALE
1 square =
2cm (³⁄₄in) square

TAB
Cut 4

Templates

The templates given on these pages are for use in the projects in this book; but they can also be helpful if you should feel inspired to make your own designs. You will find here a selection of outlines for each of the Teletubbies together with some other objects from the Tubbytronic Superdome.

To change the size of any of the outlines the easiest way is by using the enlarging or reducing facility on a photocopier. Alternatively, use the square method. This is also the method that is used for the pattern pieces that accompany several of the projects in the book.

Enlarging an outline using the square method

1 The scale of each pattern piece is marked on the grids, eg 1 square = 1cm (½in) square or 1 square = 2cm (¾in) square. Buy or draw an appropriate sized piece of squared paper, ie with squares that are 1cm (½in) or 2cm (¾in) in size.

2 Using a pencil, transfer the pattern pieces from the small grid to the larger one. Make sure you draw over the same number of squares and you will then have the correctly sized pattern from which to work.

3 If there is more than one pattern piece, write the name of each and any cutting instructions, eg cut two, foldline, on to each one to act as a reminder. Also mark any notches and their letters (if there are any).

4 Cut out the pattern pieces and use them in conjunction with the making instructions.

Note: *If you want to use this method to enlarge any of the templates on the following pages, simply draw your own grid over the top and then transfer the outline to a suitably sized larger (or smaller) one.*

Tinky Winky

Dipsy

Laa-Laa

Po

Accessories

Useful Addresses

Suppliers

Fred Aldous
37 Lever Street,
Manchester M60 1UX
telephone: 0161 236 2477
fax: 0161 236 6075
Mail order craft supplies

Art Express
12-20 Westfield Road
Leeds
W. Yorks LS3 1DF
telephone: 0800 731 4185
fax: 0113 243 6074
Mail order art and craft supplies

J W Bollom
Head Office
PO Box 78
Croydon Road
Beckenham
Kent BR3 4BL
telephone: 0181 658 2299
Felt in 84 colours, sold by the metre (yard), but ask them for non-FR felt (flameproofed) as FR coating is toxic; ring for regional branches

Borowick Fabrics Ltd
16 Berwick Street
London W1
telephone: 0171 437 2180
Speciality and theatrical fabrics such as silver and PVC

Dylon International
Worsley Bridge Road
Lower Sydenham
London SE26 5HD
telephone: 0181 663 4296
Dylon Image Maker

The Kite Store
48 Neal Street
London WC2
telephone: 0171 836 1666
Ripstop nylon (mail order)

Kleins
5 Noel Street
London W1
telephone: 0171 437 6162
e-mail: info@kleins.co.uk
web site: kleins.co.uk
Trimmings and craft supplies (mail order available)

Leaf International
http://www.leaf-international.co.uk
Website for Teletubby merchandise including stickers used in the Countdown Calendar

John Lewis Partnership
Cavendish Square
Oxford Street
London W1
telephone: 0171 629 7711
Fabric, haberdashery and craft supplies; ring for regional branches

Paperchase
213 Tottenham Court Road
London W1
telephone: 0171 580 8496
Paper and art supplies; ring for regional branches

Specialist makers

Margaret Docherty
Ruskin Mill Workshops
Old Bristol Road
Nailsworth
Glos GL6 0LA
telephone: 01453 836573
Rag rug-making tools, videos, kits, workshops, commissions

Claire Francis
Salt Cellar Hats
Salt Cellar Workshops
Salt Cellar Road
Porthleven
Cornwall
telephone: 01326 565707
Hat maker

Gill Ford
107A Malden Road
London NW5 4HR
telephone: 0171 485 1466
Paint effects and stencils

Author's Acknowledgments

Many thanks to Gill McFarland, Gill Ford, Kirsty Fox, Gill Frost, Margaret Docherty, Jenn Gilbert and Claire Francis for their help on various projects and to Sharon Turvey for the wonderful cake. Thanks to the children of Purple Class at Canonbury Infant School and Annie Turner for drawing lots of Teletubby pictures for me. Thanks also to Seline Allen for her house; and to Amari, Flynn, Holly, Kaya and Tiggy for modelling.

Other Teletubby titles available

Over the hills and far away, Teletubbies come to play! An exciting range of videos, books and audio tapes, including the following titles, are available from all good retailers.

VIDEOS

Nursery Rhymes	£9.99
Favourite Things	£9.99
Teletubbies Christmas	£9.99
Happy Christmas from the Teletubbies	£9.99
Uh-Oh! Messes and Muddles	£9.99

ACTIVITY BOOKS

Dipsy's Hat	£1.99
Laa Laa's Song	£1.99
Po's Blowy Day	£1.99
Tinky Winky's Walk	£1.99

STORY BOOKS

Dipsy Dances	£2.50
Four Happy Teletubbies	£2.50
Po Po Fast and Slow	£2.50
The Tubby Custard Mess	£2.50
Sleep Well Teletubbies	£2.50
Taking Turns	£2.50
Be Quiet Po !	£2.50
The Guitar	£2.50

BOOK & TAPE SET

Teletubbies: Time for Tubbyrobics	£4.99

NOVELTY BOOKS

Teletubby Bath Book – Puddle Indoors	£3.99
Teletubby Toast Number Board Book: Five Slices of Tubby Toast	£5.99
Teletubby Lift the Flap Book: Po's Magic Watering Can	£3.50
Teletubby Lift the Flap Book: The Noo-Noo Tidies Up	£3.50

BOOK & FRAME SETS

Po's Book of Red	£4.99
Dipsy's Book of Green	£4.99
Laa Laa's Book of Yellow	£4.99
Tinky Winky's of Purple	£4.99

STICKER BOOKS

The Teletubbyland Sticker Book	£2.99
The Tubbytronic Superdome Sticker Book	£2.99